BUILDING MORE CLASSIC GARDEN FURNITURE

Danny Proulx

POPULAR WOODWORKING BOOKS
CINCINNATI, OHIO
www.popularwoodworking.com

READ THIS IMPORTANT SAFETY NOTICE

To prevent accidents, keep safety in mind while you work. Use the safety guards installed on power equipment; they are for your protection. When working on power equipment, keep fingers away from saw blades, wear safety goggles to prevent injuries from flying wood chips and sawdust, wear headphones to protect your hearing, and consider installing a dust vacuum to reduce the amount of airborne sawdust in your woodshop. Don't wear loose clothing, such as neckties or shirts with loose sleeves, or jewelry, such as rings, necklaces or bracelets, when working on power equipment. Tie back long hair to prevent it from getting caught in your equipment. People who are sensitive to certain chemicals should check the chemical content of any product before using it. The authors and editors who compiled this book have tried to make the contents as accurate and correct as possible. Plans, illustrations, photographs and text have been carefully checked. All instructions, plans and projects should be carefully read, studied and understood before beginning construction. Due to the variability of local conditions, construction materials, skill levels, etc., neither the author nor Popular Woodworking Books assumes any responsibility for any accidents, injuries, damages or other losses incurred resulting from the material presented in this book.

METRIC CONVERSION CHART

to convert	to	multiply by
Inches	Centimeters	2.54
Centimeters	Inches	0.4
Feet	Centimeters	30.5
Centimeters	Feet	0.03
Yards	Meters	0.9
Meters	Yards	1.1
Sq. Inches	Sq. Centimeters	6.45
Sq. Centimeters	Sq. Inches	0.16
Sq. Feet	Sq. Meters	0.09
Sq. Meters	Sq. Feet	10.8
Sq. Yards	Sq. Meters	0.8
Sq. Meters	Sq. Yards	1.2
Pounds	Kilograms	0.45
Kilograms	Pounds	2.2
Ounces	Grams	28.4
Grams	Ounces	0.04

Building More Classic Garden Furniture. Copyright © 2000 by Danny Proulx. Manufactured in China. All rights reserved. No part of this book may be reproduced in any form or by any electronic or mechanical means including information storage and retrieval systems without permission in writing from the publisher, except by a reviewer, who may quote brief passages in a review. Published by Popular Woodworking Books, an imprint of F&W Publications, Inc., 4700 East Galbraith Road, Cincinnati, Ohio, 45236. First edition.

Visit our Web site at www.popularwoodworking.com for information on more resources for woodworkers.

Other fine Popular Woodworking Books are available from your local bookstore or direct from the publisher.

06 05 04 03 02   6 5 4 3 2

Library of Congress Cataloging-in-Publication Data

Proulx, Danny, 1947–
   Building more classic garden furniture.-- 1st ed.
      p. cm.
   ISBN 1-55870-564-3 (alk. paper)
   1. Outdoor furniture. 2. Furniture making. 3. Garden ornaments and furniture. I. Title.

TT197.5.O9 P74   2000
684.1'8--dc21   00-060675

Edited by Michael Berger
Production edited by Jennifer Churchill
Designed by Brian Roeth
Production coordinated by Emily Gross
Computer illustrations by Len Churchill, Lenmark Communications Ltd., Alden Rd., Markham, Ontario (905) 475-5222
Step-by-step photography by Danny Proulx
Cover and chapter lead photography by Michael Bowie, Lux Photographic Services, Lancaster Rd., Ottawa, Ontario (613) 247-7199

ABOUT THE AUTHOR

Danny Proulx is a monthly columnist for *CabinetMaker Magazine.* He has contributed freelance articles for *Canadian Woodworking, Canadian Home Workshop, Popular Woodworking* and *Woodshop News* magazines. He is the author of *Build Your Own Kitchen Cabinets, The Kitchen Cabinetmaker's Building and Business Manual, How to Build Classic Garden Furniture, Smart Shelving and Storage Solutions, Fast and Easy Techniques for Building Modern Cabinetry,* and *Building Cabinet Doors and Drawers.* His Web site is www.cabinetmaking.com; his e-mail is danny@cabinetmaking.com.

ACKNOWLEDGEMENTS

I have been fortunate to work with many suppliers and manufacturers while writing this book. They have supplied products, technical literature and material. I have listed them in the "Sources" section of this book. I recommend them without hesitation and ask that you take a look at what they offer.

I would also like to offer special thanks to Trudic Lentz of Russell, Ontario. Her amazing garden was the backdrop for all the chapter and cover photographs. This fantastic creative space full of color and aroma enhanced my work.

DEDICATION

A writer often creates the written work alone. But dozens of support and research partners help out. Without them, many of these works wouldn't achieve any level of quality. I'm very fortunate to have the best "team" in the business.

My wife, Gale, is always there to help, advise and offer alternatives. She is my first, and most demanding, critic. My assistant on many of the projects is Jack Chaters, who is always ready to go when something needs doing. Michael Bowie of Lux Photography in Ottawa, Ontario, is by far the most talented and creative photographer I've ever worked with. The graphics are created by Len Churchill of Lenmark Communications in Markham, Ontario. He makes Illustrator software do things Adobe didn't know could be done. He is richly talented.

Finally, to all the other team members — I couldn't have done it without your support. Thank you.

table of contents

PROJECTS

PROJECT ONE
horizontal panel planter
16

PROJECT TWO
elegant planter
22

PROJECT THREE
planter bench
28

PROJECT FOUR
corner privacy screen
34

PROJECT FIVE
classic garden bench
40

PROJECT SIX
curved planter bench
48

PROJECT SEVEN
folding side table
56

PROJECT EIGHT
outdoor coffee table
62

PROJECT NINE
formal side table
68

PROJECT TEN
tête-à-tête bench
76

PROJECT ELEVEN
outdoor dining set
84

PROJECT TWELVE
classic picnic table
92

PROJECT THIRTEEN
octagonal picnic table
98

PROJECT FOURTEEN
chaise lounge
108

PROJECT FIFTEEN
hammock stand
118

introduction   *page 6*

construction techniques   *page 8*

sources   *page 126*

index   *page 127*

Warm weather allows us to enjoy the great outdoors. That special time is important to all of us, but even more precious for those of us who live in the northern climates. We're like a pack of bears, emerging from hibernation as the warm weather descends. Those long, hard, cold winters make summer especially enjoyable.

Our backyards have become extended living spaces. Many of us have decks, patios and gardens to enjoy. Some of us may just be starting to plan our outdoor living spaces. But, regardless of the situation, we all want good-looking, functional furniture to use and to beautify our homes and gardens.

I enjoy spending time in my shop, designing and building outdoor projects: garden structures, planters, chairs and tables. These and other projects for the backyard foster a lot of creative freedom. We don't have to hide every joint, sand and polish until the piece resembles glass or follow any standards. Freedom of expression rules.

If you're like me, building outdoor woodworking projects is much like being a bus driver who takes a bus-tour holiday. It has many of the same disciplines, but it's somehow refreshing and different. Building outdoor projects is a "holiday" for me, even though I'm in the workshop every day. I'm a cabinetmaker by trade, but I have a sense of freedom to create when I'm making something for the garden or the deck.

We do, however, have to consider one big unknown — Mother Nature. She has very little respect for our handiwork, so we must take special precautions to protect and preserve each piece. Sun, wind, rain and shifting temperatures can destroy even the finest project. Fortunately, protective finishes have progressed in recently, so we can now enjoy our work for years.

The reason I write these books is because I love working with wood. And I don't claim to know everything about the subject. More importantly, I don't write just to show people how much I know. In fact, I learn new things about woodworking every day — even after 30 years of gluing sticks together.

In each project, I will attempt to highlight one joint, construction technique or assembly process. I'll show you one technique, which is often the simplest, and try to suggest other routes to achieve the same end result; but you don't have to build it my way. There are dozens of possible variations. I'll do my best to share the options that exist for each project.

As I've said in previous books, if you follow the plans and build the project, you will end up with a project that will survive a few years. If you learn something or experiment with each project, you will gain knowledge that will last a lifetime. Have fun, experiment and don't be afraid to make a mistake!

construction techniques

We must take special precautions when building outdoor wood furniture. Unprotected wood, when exposed to all the elements of rain, wind and sun, will rot in a fairly short time. Some woods are more resistant to outdoor conditions than others, but for the most part, they should all be protected in certain ways so their maximum useful life is achieved. The type of wood, the hardware used to connect the pieces and the protective coatings applied are important issues to consider.

THE PROPERTIES OF WOOD

The first decision to make when building outdoor furniture is which type of wood to use. Softwoods such as redwood and cedar, as well as some hardwoods including mahogany, white oak and teak, have long been considered good "outdoor woods." These three hardwoods have been used in the boat-building industry for years. And although the cost of these woods will impact your decision, it shouldn't be the most important issue. An inexpensive wood that will quickly rot outdoors is not cost-effective.

Board Foot and Grading

Lumber is usually sold by the board foot. Or at least, the price shown on a piece of lumber is based on a board foot price. A board foot is a piece of lumber 1" thick by 12" wide by 12" long. When calculating the number of board feet required for a project, multiply the board's thickness in inches by the width in inches by the length in feet, and divide by twelve.

There is a grading system for lumber, and you'll often see terms like *select* and *common* grades. If you're not familiar with the grading system in your area, acquire the government grading regulations brochure. It will be time well spent. Details, such as defects allowed, moisture content and species, are often contained in the ratings.

Green Wood vs. Dry Wood

A tree's weight is made up of a high proportion of water. Boards just cut from the tree are "wet" and are referred to as green lumber. You can imagine the problems that would be created if we joined lumber with a high moisture content. Joints, such as the common mortise-and-tenon, would more than likely fail as the wood dries.

Because of problems like these, it's best to purchase kiln-dried lumber with a moisture content of 15% or less. Lumber of this type is reasonably stable, because most of the shrinking is complete.

But we're not limited to buying only expensive kiln-dried lumber for these projects. You can use construction-grade or S-green (sawn green) wood with a bit of planning. New wood, if not kiln dried, should have ample time to dry out. Unassembled boards should be air-dried for four to six weeks in warm, dry weather. Place spacers in each layer so that air can circulate and dry the wood. If rain is forecast, cover the wood.

Safety Issues

Consider safety when working with wood. One issue, referred to as *toxic reactions of wood*, should be studied by all woodworkers. Certain woods are more toxic than others, and not everyone reacts in the same manner. Most libraries have books that deal with this subject, and I advise everyone to read and understand the issues.

SPECIES OF WOOD

We'll be dealing with two types of wood for the projects in this book — softwoods and hardwoods. In general, softwoods (from conifers) grow faster and are therefore less expensive than hardwoods (which come from deciduous trees). And though two of the softwoods, namely cedar and redwood, are slow-growing, their resistance to outdoor conditions justifies the higher cost.

Cedar

Cedar is classified as a softwood with very desirable decay-resistant properties. Generally known as western red cedar or eastern white cedar, its color ranges from a light tan to a dark red.

Cedar is easy to work with, and while not exceptionally strong, it's more than acceptable for most outdoor furniture projects. In some parts of North America, it's the wood of choice for decks, picnic tables and fences.

With the exception of pressure-treated wood, cedar is the least expensive of the woods used for outdoor projects. But be sure to choose boards that are relatively free of knots. When you're pricing cedar, be certain you inquire

about the grade classification. *Number one common* cedar will be cheaper than *select A* cedar, but will have a difference in appearance, as well.

In general, particularly when cost is a major concern, cedar is a good choice. And if you are able to select the wood at the lumberyard, you'll find many usable pieces of wood in the common grade. With selective picking and careful cutting, cedar will meet most of your requirements.

Redwood

Thirty years ago, redwood was plentiful and relatively inexpensive. It was the choice wood for outdoor projects and was commonly used for house siding. Today, however, the government protects this western coastal wood, and production is strictly controlled. It tends to be expensive and hard to get on the East Coast of North America. If you live on the West Coast, you may find this desirable softwood reasonably priced and therefore a good choice for your projects.

Redwood is soft and easy to work, but care must be taken to avoid splintering. It has a beautiful red color and is extremely decay resistant.

More information on this wood, its properties and grading procedures, as well as suggested applications, is available from the California Redwood Association: (888) 225-7339 or www.calredwood.org.

Mahogany

Three types of mahogany are commonly available — Honduras, African and Philippine. The first two are used in furniture construction, while the coarse, open-grained Philippine mahogany is often used for interior doors and trim work.

Decay resistant and longtime favorites of boatbuilders, Honduras and African mahogany have beautiful color and texture. This hardwood is ideal for building outdoor furniture and is often very reasonably priced.

The board foot price varies, depending on your area's supply and demand.

You have many choices when it comes to which lumber to use for your outdoor projects, and each type of lumber will lend its own unique color. Shown here, left to right: white oak, mahogany, redwood, pressure-treated yellow pine, cedar and teak.

You may also find that the names are different which can make it difficult to determine just what you're getting. Honduras mahogany is called *genuine* or *Central American* in some areas. However, the goal is to buy a furniture-grade wood with properties that are found in the Honduras mahogany.

Teak
Teak feels oily and has a very high level of silica. Therefore, carbide cutting tools are a necessity when working this wood. It ranges in color from a yellow-brown to dark brown. Teak is a durable wood and dimensionally stable.

Metal, in contact with teak, does not cause rust marks on the wood. That trait makes it perfect for outdoor furniture. It is, however, increasingly rare and very expensive. The decision on whether or not to use teak depends on the project you're going to build. If a garden bench, constructed of teak, provides 20 years of useful service, that cost over the 20-year period is not hard to bear. If the bench lasts only a couple of years, then it is an expensive proposition.

White Oak
White oak's sapwood is white and the heartwood is light brown. Boatbuilders, as well as coopers, have long favored this wood. The heartwood pores are filled with a natural membrane called tyloses, which makes the white oak virtually impenetrable by water. The natural expansion of wood when wet, coupled with white oak's high level of tyloses, is why this wood is favored for making casks. Once filled with wine or spirits, they will not leak.

But since white oak is widely used, it's in high demand and supply can't always keep up; consequently, white oak is very expensive.

If you have access to a white oak tree lot, it would be a good choice for garden furniture as long as it is finished properly. If you have to buy it at the retail rate, it may be more economical to use another hardwood.

Pressure-Treated Wood
Pressure-treated wood is becoming more popular for outdoor construction projects. It's inexpensive and many manufacturers warranty the product for up to 30 years if properly installed.

Spruce, pine and fir are commonly used. The wood is dehydrated under a vacuum and impregnated with preservatives leaving the fibers unpalatable to fungi and insects. The wood is stamped with letters designating the type of chemical applied, most often chromated copper arsenate (CCA) and other copper arsenates and chromates.

The treated wood can be cut and fastened like any other wood, but give spe-

cial attention to the fact that chemicals are present. It's advisable to read the manufacturer's safety guidelines before working with this product.

Often green or tan in color, pressure-treated wood can usually be painted. If left "natural," most will turn a silver gray color. Verify that the pressure-treated wood you purchase can be painted.

Plastic "Wood"
There's a new player on the outdoor-furniture and deck-building scene. It's a woodlike product made from recycled plastics and formed into common lumber sizes. The product has been used in Europe since 1980, and the reports from consumers have been positive. Many manufacturers will warranty that plastic wood will not split, crack or splinter for periods of up to 50 years. Engineering reports say the product will last for 400 years without any noticeable degradation. That's an impressive statistic, but I don't believe I'll have to worry about that.

Plastic wood is high-density polyethylene (HDPE) with pigments and ultraviolet (UV) inhibitors. It's ideal when projects will be in constant contact with the ground, because it won't rot.

Plastic wood is nonporous, won't absorb water and can be worked like standard lumber. It can be cut, drilled, routed, screwed and nailed using regular woodworking tools. However, I would strongly recommend you use carbide-tipped cutting tools. And since plastic wood will expand and contract, check with the supplier of your material for the specifications and any precautions to be used when building your project.

Many manufacturers of plastic wood say that predrilling for screws is not necessary, but I disagree. Drilling a pilot hole for screws always guarantees improved performance.

One major advantage of plastic wood is that it's colored throughout. Therefore, staining or finishing of any type isn't necessary. The projects I've built in the past haven't faded, so it appears to be the answer for those of us who aren't

Working With Pine

Now, after going through all the wood types and finishing principles, I'm going to contradict myself. I believe that you can use any wood outside with success. But that statement is heavily weighted with a precaution: The wood must be properly protected.

To illustrate my point, I've used pine outdoors on many, many occasions, and those structures are still serving me well. How do you achieve these successful results? Simply make certain that all wood surfaces are coated with a protective wood preservative.

Protecting all surfaces means using a clear wood preservative after all parts are cut to size, prior to joining. In many cases rot, caused by moisture and mildew, tends to happen at the spot where two boards are joined. There is often a lack of air circulation, and wood on the joint surfaces is left unprotected. Bare wood, no matter the species, won't stand up very long under those conditions. I would agree that some woods, such as teak, are naturally resistant, but a little extra insurance is always the best policy. Make it a practice to use a clear protective coating on all surfaces and you'll extend the wood's life greatly. As well, applying a little extra to the joint areas will go a long way to help in preventing damage.

Cut and sand all parts, then liberally apply a clear wood preservative to all surfaces. When using pine for outdoor structures, be certain the wood's moisture content is below 18%. Assemble the project, then coat with a protective translucent finish for exterior wood. You can use any quality finish such as the Sikkens or Olympic products.

Many pleasing colors are available nowadays. You can use a mahogany finish on pine with dramatic results. As always, test the finishes completely before committing to the final coat.

Most clear protective exterior penetrating finishes will allow you to apply a stained finish. But it's worth repeating. Make sure all the products are compatible.

I'll detail the finish on each project. And to illustrate the different combinations, I will use various woods and stains. Your choice on which to use is a matter of personal taste. But the protection process is mandatory if you want many years of enjoyable service from the outdoor projects you create.

fans of staining and painting. And many manufacturers guarantee the color retention properties.

Plastic wood is available in all the common lumber sizes. But there is a grade, or type, difference with some manufacturers, and all of the plastic wood available today isn't made the same way. There are wood-plastic mixes, fiberglass-reinforced material and other types of strengthened products.

One concern with plastic wood is that some of the product available today is not suitable for long spans. That's the reason a reinforced material is offered as well as the mix-type products. But that limitation is a minor issue, providing you are well informed. Ask your supplier for the span tables with the material you purchase.

Before you build any of the projects in this book with plastic wood, research the material you plan to buy. If all your

questions are answered, and you believe the specifications will meet or exceed the demands, buy the material. You'll find it is a pleasure to build with and pays dividends because of its no-maintenance feature.

HARDWARE

One major enemy of outdoor furniture is the metal fastener. Steel or common zinc-plated screws react with the tannic acids in the wood causing dark stains and streaks. I've taken apart wood decks that were full of rot and weakened by steel screws and bolts. Do not, under any circumstances, use fastening hardware made of unprotected steel, including zinc-plated hardware.

Hot-Dipped Galvanized
Screws and bolts treated by the hot-dipped galvanized method are specifically designed for outdoor use.

Electroplated galvanized hardware doesn't seem to hold up as well as hot-dipped galvanized hardware. Zinc is used as the coating in both methods, and acts as a barrier against the tannic acid in the wood.

Stainless Steel
Fasteners made from iron with chrome and nickel added are known as stainless steel. They are the most rust-resistant screws and bolts available. And they are the most expensive.

Stainless fasteners are hard and ideally suited for outdoor furniture construction. The high price can sometimes be prohibitive, but using these screws will add years of life to your furniture. In that regard, they are a small investment that will pay dividends in the long run.

Outdoor Screws
In the last few years, many hardware manufacturers have introduced a line of outdoor fastening products. Outdoor screws are commonly green-, gray- or bronze-colored, and they can be found in the deck-building sections of many hardware stores.

Often these screws are ceramic, coated or plated with a rust preventative to delay the metal reacting with wood acids. I've used these screws on a few outdoor projects, and they seem to stand up well. However, check the supply in your area, compare the cost against the stainless steel version and see if there is a substantial difference. If there is a big difference, it may be worthwhile to use the coated hardware. Study the specification data for these products to determine if they are suitable for your application.

OUTDOOR GLUES
Glue, in combination with a mechanically sound joint, is the heart of your construction project. Outdoor furniture has some special considerations that must be accounted for when constructing your project.

Outdoor glues must retain their bonding properties under very adverse conditions. Water is the most destructive element these projects will face, so the adhesives must be waterproof.

In the past, the standard outdoor glues were two-part epoxy or plastic resins. In recent years, a few manufacturers have developed one-part glues that are now considered acceptable general-purpose adhesives for outdoor furniture projects.

Aliphatic Resin Glue

The most recent one-part glues to be introduced are the polyaliphatic resins. One, called Titebond II, has been in common use for the last few years.

It's a yellow polyaliphatic resin glue that forms a Type II bond, meaning it has to pass specific water-soak tests and continue to retain its shear strength. These glues are designed for use above the waterline and therefore could not be used on boats where the joint is submersed in water.

I've used this adhesive as a general-purpose outdoor glue for various furniture projects, and it appears to hold up well. If conditions are extremely wet for continued periods of time, it may be worth considering some of the other waterproof epoxy glues. But under normal conditions, these easy-to-use, one-part glues are suitable for all your

projects. And they're inexpensive, compared to the two-part epoxies and resin adhesives.

Polyurethane Glue

Franklin International has introduced a glue called Titebond Polyurethane Glue, and the Borden Company markets the Elmer's Probond brand. They're reported to be 100% waterproof and are thick one-part glues ideal for outdoor furniture projects.

Polyurethane glues are not intended for use below the waterline or continued submersion. They're recommended for wood, ceramics and plastic bonding. The shear strength on hard maple has been tested at over 3,500 pounds per square inch for each of these glues.

This is another of the many advances in one-part outdoor glues that have been developed in the last few years. These advances have simplified the building of outdoor projects when you compare these products to the two-part epoxy systems that were the norm in the past.

Plastic Resin Marine Glue

Normally, this adhesive is a urea-formaldehyde powder that must be mixed with water. It was considered to be the standard glue for marine and out-

door construction projects.

Two-part resins are more difficult to use because you must mix only the amount you'll use in a reasonable length of time. In that respect, there is the waste factor to consider, compared to the ready-to-use aliphatic or polyurethane glues.

There are some drawbacks to using plastic resins, including the urea gas given off while the glue is curing. Additionally, they cure at room temperature, so you need a heated shop.

Like many adhesives, plastic resins don't fill gaps very well, so joints must be well fitted. And oily woods, such as teak, don't bond well with plastic resin.

Epoxy Resin

When a high-strength, highly waterproof bond is needed, epoxy resin is the adhesive of choice. Most manufacturers sell a two-part system consisting of a resin and hardener.

However, epoxy resin can be very frustrating to use. For all its positive aspects, including high shear strength and almost-completely waterproof properties, it has some negative aspects that must be considered.

Epoxy cures fast, and if glue squeezes out during the joint fitting, it has to be removed immediately or it's there for

When purchasing hardware, remember to choose a type that will resist the weather well in your part of the country. Shown here are samples of stainless steel, hot-dipped galvanized and coated outdoor screws.

You have just as many choices for adhesives as you do for wood species. Choose a glue that will best meet the needs of your specific project. Shown here, left to right: polyaliphatic resin glue for outdoor projects, powdered resin, polyurethane and regular yellow wood glue (aliphatic resin).

Sanding and Finishing Tips

Here are a few sanding and finishing tips that may improve the looks of your project:
- Sand immediately before wood finishing, if possible.
- The coarser the sandpaper grits used, the darker the stain color produced, due to penetration.
- Use caution when working with a belt sander, as a worn belt will polish the wood surface. Worn belts can also cause intense heat that will burn the wood, which may restrict finish penetration.
- To avoid scratches on wood, use a series of grits with the next only one grade finer than the previous. For example, a sanding sequence could be 100, 120 and, finally, 140.
- Sand new wood with an open-coat-type paper made with silicon carbide or aluminum oxide. Use silicon papers for sanding between finishes.
- Sanding not only smooths the wood, it prepares the wood for finish by creating an anchor for the coating.

good. Don't get any on your shop equipment, including wood clamps that are temporarily holding the joint, because it won't come off easily. And the price is high. A 40-ounce kit can cost as much as $40.

Construction Adhesives

Over the last few years, I've used some of the latest exterior construction adhesives. They are sold in cans or caulking gun tubes. In general, I've found them to be more than satisfactory for many outdoor building projects.

I normally use adhesives sold in tubes for use with my caulking gun because they are simple to apply and are inexpensive when compared to some of the other exterior glues. Look for the best ratings possible and follow the manufacturer's instructions.

Glue Choices

When considering all the glues available today, I've opted for the polyurethane glues or the exterior construction adhesives. They have some disadvantages; they don't have the high waterproof ratings of the resin and epoxy glues. But for general-purpose outdoor furniture under normal conditions, these one-part glues and construction adhesives are more than acceptable. They've progressed a great deal in the last few years.

For your own peace of mind, look at the general weather conditions in your

area and study the adhesive's ratings applicable to those conditions. In most cases, the one-part glues will serve your purposes.

FINISHING OUTDOOR PROJECTS

Concern for the environment has forced many manufacturers to develop more environmentally friendly exterior wood finishes. Just as weather conditions vary in each area, so does the concern for the level of protection required. Because the laws are different from region to region, it's difficult to recommend one all-around finish.

Many regions have laws limiting the volatile organic compounds (VOC) given off by exterior wood coatings. Because of these new laws, manufacturers are, and have been, developing new products to meet the standards. The changes are rapid and numerous, so keeping track of the new coatings available is a difficult job.

In general terms, no matter where you live, one problem you'll encounter is discoloration of wood. Ultraviolet light (radiation) breaks down the surface cells in the lumber and turns most species gray. Therefore, we need a finish that has a UV blocker to maintain the wood's natural color.

That's the first issue.

Secondly, no matter what product you use, refinishing every few years will

be necessary. I don't believe there's an exterior finish made that will last more than five years under the most ideal conditions.

The two main categories of exterior finishes are penetrating stains and surface coatings. However, recent environmental legislation has caused manufacturers to try new formulas. These include water-based and water-oil-modified formulations, as well as attempts to increase the solids in an oil-based coating.

One general rule for exterior wood finishes is to use a penetrating stain. Surface coatings, such as paint or varnish, will eventually blister and peel. While penetrating stains fade and become weathered, they don't blister. It's simpler to sand and refinish a stain finish, because you don't have to scrape and sand the blistered coatings.

There are many exterior penetrating finishes on the market. They are often called water-repellent exterior stains or wood protectors.

To enhance the natural color of the wood, use a clear finish. If you want to change the color of the wood slightly while enhancing the grain, use a transparent or semitransparent exterior stain.

Finishing Do's and Don'ts

Try to apply all finishes when the temperature is between 10°C/50°F and 35°C/95°F. Temperatures, either too hot or too cold, can have a negative effect on the final finish.

Be certain to saturate all end grains, and apply liberal coats of finish to the wood. Try to maintain a wet edge when using any finish, and coat in the direction of the grain.

Do not apply finishes in direct sunlight or when the surface is hot to the touch. If dew or frost is present, many stains will not work properly. Applying any coating in wet weather can result in a poor finish, with moisture trapped in the wood.

As a general rule, I suggest that you not apply any finishes to wood that has a moisture content higher than 18%.

There are many manufacturers in the marketplace and most have very good products. Read the available literature offered by those companies and study their warranty programs. If possible, find someone who has used a finish you like on outdoor furniture, to determine how it's held up to local weather conditions.

JOINERY TECHNIQUES

It isn't our intention to teach wood joinery in this book. Volumes could be written on just this subject alone. *Good Wood Joints* by Albert Jackson and David Day (Popular Woodworking Books, 2000) is an excellent resource for wood joinery information. However, be aware that we will detail the joinery for each project.

Most experienced woodworkers have made many of the joints used throughout this book. Lap, mortise-and-tenon, dowel and dado joints are a few of the common methods of joining wood that we'll use. But in general, the mortise-and-tenon, or one of its many variations, will be featured and used when building the projects.

Mortise-and-Tenon Joints

This joint has been used for centuries as the standard method of attaching two pieces of wood. It's most often used to attach wood together at right angles.

This joint gets its mechanical strength from one piece of wood being fitted into another, with glue and fasteners. There are many variations of the mortise-and-tenon, and as many rules for joint sizes.

One rule, which many people follow, is that the thickness of the tenon should equal one-third the width of the stock. For example, two 1½" pieces of wood, joined at right angles, will have a ½" tenon.

For the majority of applications, leaving a ⅛" shoulder around the tenon, and then making the mortise to fit, normally provides a solid, mechanically sound joint. The joint should fit securely, but still allow room for glue. If you have to hammer the mortise and tenon together, it's too tight.

These joints can be cut by hand, on a table saw and drill press, or with a table saw and mortise drill press equipped with a mortising chisel. It doesn't matter how you make the joint, as long as it's secure.

Dado Joints

A dado joint is best cut with either a router or carbide dado blade assembly on a table saw. It is a simple joint to make, and one that most everyone has mastered.

This joint is a slot that joins two pieces of wood, often at right angles. As with all other joints, it should be snug without binding.

Biscuit Joints

Over the last few years, biscuit joinery has gained tremendous popularity. Biscuit joiners allow the woodworker to make a quick, clean, accurate joint. A biscuit cut from beech wood is inserted into the slot, and when glue is applied, the biscuit swells, tightening the bond.

Biscuit joinery has many applications, but is well suited to strengthening miter joints. It is also good for butt joinery, particularly for panel glue-ups.

The cutting tool (called a biscuit joiner) is reasonably priced. Most woodworkers will find that this tool is a handy addition to their shop.

Other Joinery

As discussed earlier, numerous joints are used throughout this book. However, none are extremely complicated. A little care and attention when cutting these joints will result in success every time.

If you're intimidated by any woodworking procedures in this book, practice on the simpler projects. Most projects, in total, look difficult. But breaking them down into small sections always simplifies the process. Practice the joinery on scrap lumber and you'll soon master all the procedures. As my wise, old, cabinetmaker father often said, "It's only a few sticks of wood glued together, making it look complicated." Concentrate on the individual sections and the whole project will come together successfully.

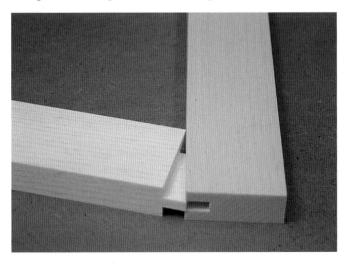

A typical mortise-and-tenon joint.

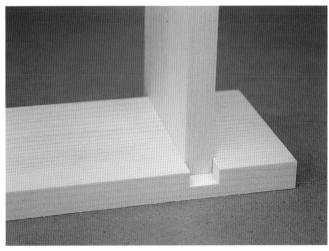

A typical dado joint.

horizontal panel planter

This project is simply a series of stacked wooden rectangles. My finished piece is about 12" x 20", but I could have made it any dimension. If you have different requirements, change the sizes so your planter will fit perfectly in that special spot.

I used pine for this project, but as I'll repeat throughout this book, any wood species can be used as long as it's properly protected.

Since the bottom board will rot over time due to the soil, water and fertilizer, use an inexpensive piece of plywood with a few drainage holes as a sacrificial bottom that can be replaced as often as needed.

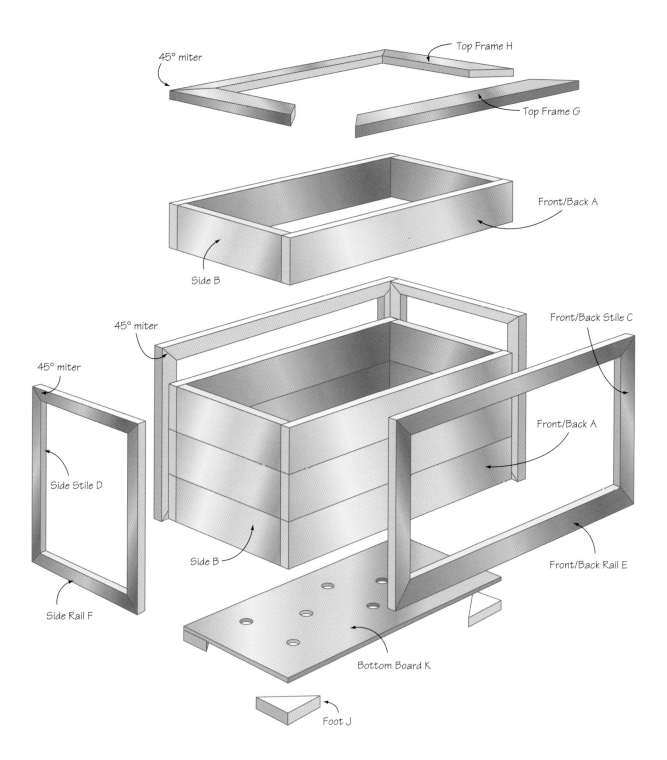

45° miter

Top Frame H

Top Frame G

Front/Back A

Side B

45° miter

Front/Back Stile C

45° miter

Front/Back A

45° miter

Side Stile D

Side B

Front/Back Rail E

Side Rail F

Bottom Board K

Foot J

CUTTING LIST • **horizontal panel planter**

REF.	QTY.	PART	MATERIAL	THICK	WIDTH	LENGTH	COMMENTS
A	8	Fronts and backs	Pine	$3/4$	$3\frac{1}{2}$	18	
B	8	Sides	Pine	$3/4$	$3\frac{1}{2}$	$10\frac{1}{2}$	
C	4	Front and back stiles	Pine	$3/4$	2	14	Mitered
D	4	Side stiles	Pine	$3/4$	$1\frac{1}{4}$	14	Mitered
E	4	Front and back rails	Pine	$3/4$	2	$19\frac{1}{2}$	Mitered
F	4	Side rails	Pine	$3/4$	$1\frac{1}{4}$	12	Mitered
G	2	Top frames	Pine	$3/4$	2	20	Mitered
H	2	Top frames	Pine	$3/4$	2	$13\frac{3}{4}$	Mitered
J	4	Feet	Pine	$3/4$	$1\frac{1}{2}$	$3\frac{1}{2}$	Mitered
K	1	Bottom board	Plywood	$1/2$	$10\frac{1}{2}$	$16\frac{1}{2}$	

Hardware and Supplies

$1\frac{1}{2}$" Galvanized finishing nails

Polyurethane glue

Paintable exterior caulk

Sikkens Cetol 1 #009 Dark Oak finish

REQUIRED tools

Table Saw or Circular Saw

Drill

Combination Square

Miter Box

Hammer

Screw Gun or Drivers

Sander or
Sandpaper and Block

Router and Bits

Tip

Round over one outside edge of
the stiles and rails before cutting
the 45° miters. This technique prevents damaging the point of the
angle cut with a router bit.

1 After cutting the eight front and back boards (A) and the eight side boards (B), join the sides to the fronts and backs using polyurethane glue and galvanized finishing nails. You should have four rectangular boxes 3½" high by 12" deep by 18" wide.

Tip

Planters come in close contact with soil and water, so the potential for wood damage is increased. If you cover the interior surfaces with heavy plastic before putting in the soil, the wood will last many years longer.

2 Apply glue to one edge of each box, align and stack them on top of each other, and clamp until secure. The stiles and rails that form the outside frame are 2" wide on the front and back and 1¼" wide on the sides. The 1¼" width of the thinner stile (D), added to the ¾" thickness of the wider stile (C), combines for a total width of 2". All sides of the frame around the box are then a total of 2" wide. Cut the wide and narrow stiles (C and D) as detailed in the materials list with a 45° miter. Glue and secure in place with galvanized finishing nails as shown in the photo above. (Note that the wider stiles overlap the narrow stile.)

Tip

Polyurethane glue that's exterior rated cures with water. Remember to wipe each piece of wood to be glued with a damp rag before applying glue. This glue is expensive, but you don't need much on each joint.

3 Cut the eight front, back and side rails (E and F). Install the wider rails (E) on the front and back of the planter. Then as shown above, use glue and galvanized finishing nails to secure the 45° rails.

4 Prior to installing the top and feet, sand all surfaces, use exterior paintable caulk to fill the nail holes, and round over the four corners with a ⅜" roundover bit in a router or by hand with sandpaper. Next, cut the top frame pieces (G and H) using a 45° miter on both ends of each board. Install the frame with glue and nails so that it hangs over all faces by about ¼". Then as shown, round over the outside and inside edge with a ⅜" router bit.

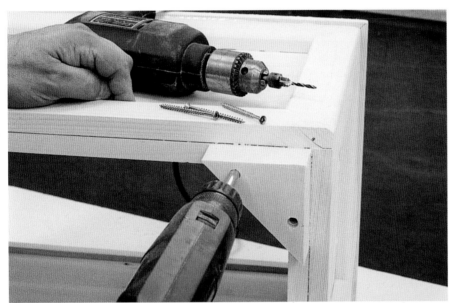

5 The four feet (J) are cut at 45° across the width of a 2×4. You'll need about 12" of stock for the feet. Attach them to the bottom of the planter with screws. Do not glue them in place, because they will eventually rot due to contact with the earth. By not gluing, the screws can be removed, allowing easy replacement.

6 The bottom (K) in my planter is a piece of ½" exterior sheeting. I always keep the scraps of sheeting material from building projects because they make inexpensive sacrificial bottoms for my planters. Drill a few drainage holes in the bottom and rest it on the four feet. Finally, sand the planter, fill any nail holes or cracks with paintable exterior caulk, and apply a good exterior finish. I used Sikkens Cetol 1 #009 Dark Oak.

Tip
One gardener friend of mine makes the bottoms with Plexiglas. It's more expensive, but they last forever.

elegant planter

Here's an easy-to-build planter that would be a great addition to any entrance. It can also be used for plants that are grown outside in the summer months but must be brought inside during the colder times. It's not necessary to fill the planter with soil; you can put a flowerpot inside the box. If you know how high the plant will be when blooming, you can adjust the baseboard level. The pot will be hidden, leaving the flowers visible.

The poster style is elegant, and just about any wood species would be suitable. I used a combination of pine and cedar. The legs are stock $1\frac{1}{2}$"-thick pine, and the sides are ready-made cedar bead board purchased at the home store.

I used a modified mortise-and-tenon joint for this project. You'll cut two grooves in each post and attach two $\frac{1}{2}$"-thick plywood panels at 90° to each other. Cut this stopped groove on a router table. If you don't own this equipment, you can drill a series of $\frac{1}{2}$" holes and chisel out the waste. It will take a little longer, but the end result is the same. The upper and lower cap rails also require a groove along one edge. Again, a router table is the ideal tool, but you can use any table saw by making multiple passes.

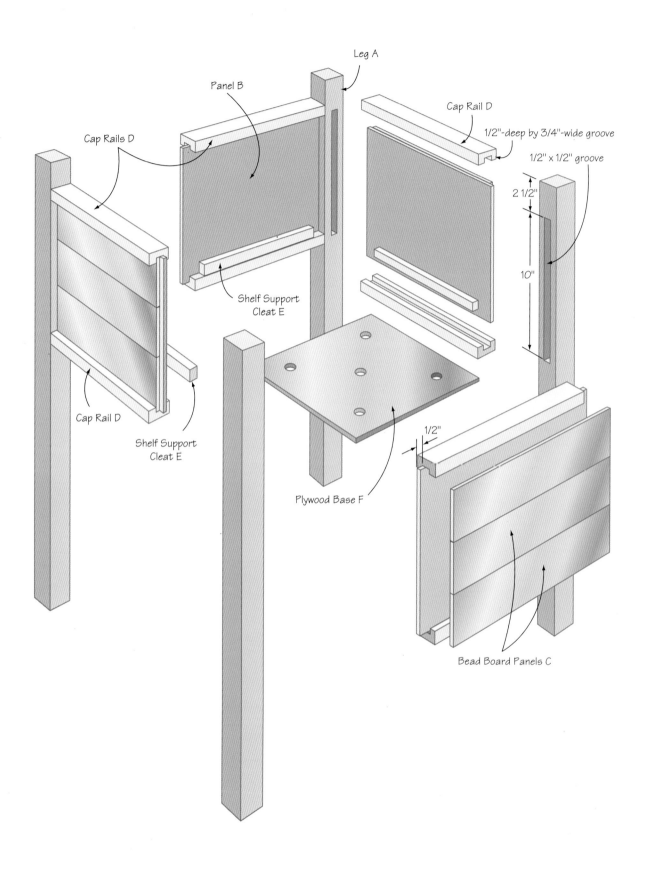

Leg A

Panel B

Cap Rails D

Cap Rail D

1/2"-deep by 3/4"-wide groove

1/2" x 1/2" groove

2 1/2"

10"

Shelf Support Cleat E

Cap Rail D

Shelf Support Cleat E

Plywood Base F

1/2"

Bead Board Panels C

CUTTING LIST • **elegant planter**

REF.	QTY.	PART	MATERIAL	THICK	WIDTH	LENGTH	COMMENTS
A	4	Legs	Pine	$1\frac{1}{2}$	$1\frac{1}{2}$	23	
B	4	Panels	Plywood	$\frac{1}{2}$	10	14	
C	12	Bead board panels	Cedar	$\frac{1}{4}$	$3\frac{1}{2}$	13	
D	8	Cap rails	Cedar	1	$1\frac{1}{2}$	13	
E	4	Shelf support cleats	Cedar	1	$\frac{3}{4}$	12	
F	1	Plywood base	Plywood	$\frac{1}{2}$	14	14	

Hardware and Supplies

$1\frac{1}{4}$" Exterior-rated screws

Finishing nails

Polyurethane glue

Sikkens Cetol 1 #045 Mahogany finish

REQUIRED **tools**

Table Saw or Circular Saw

Drill

Combination Square

Hammer

Screw Gun or Drivers

Sander or Sandpaper and Block

Router and Bits

1 Each leg requires two stopped grooves on adjoining faces. A stopped groove doesn't go all the way through to each end of the board. It has to be plunged into the router bit at one end and raised out of the bit at the other end. Each cut is ½" wide by ½" deep by 10" long and is centered on the leg face. So after cutting the legs (A) to length as listed in the cutting list, begin the plunge cut 2½" down from the top of each leg. Place reference marks on the router table for the plunge-and-remove action so all the cuts are equally placed.

2 Cut the four plywood panels (B) to size. Before inserting them in the leg grooves, square the rounded ends of each groove with a chisel. Then install the panels with glue and clamp until the adhesive cures.

Tip

You can further strengthen the panel-to-leg joints by installing pins — small brads driven through the leg into the panel at the joint. Drive them from the inside so they won't be visible.

3 You have a couple of options at this point. You can paint the panels, possibly a contrasting color to the legs, or cover the panels with thin cedar siding boards as I have. These are tongue-and-groove bead boards (C) that are nailed in place through the tongue. It's not always possible to fit three full boards on the panel, so trim either the top or bottom flush with the plywood panel.

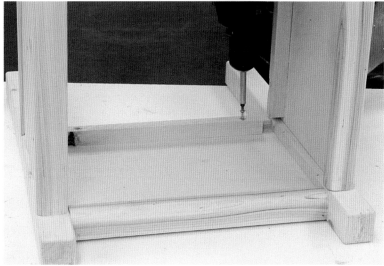

5 Attach the four shelf support cleats (E) to the panels with glue and 1¼" screws. They can be installed at any height you require.

Tip

Don't cut the grooves in the cap rails until you install the decorative bead boards. Mine were almost ¼" thick, but yours may be different. Measure the thickness and adjust the cap rail groove width to fit snugly over the side panels and boards.

4 Cap the top and bottom edge of each panel with a piece of cedar. Cut a ¾"-wide by ½"-deep groove, centered on one face of each cap rail (D). The groove is located on one of the 1½" faces. Then put glue in each groove and clamp in place until dry. Or use finishing nails driven at an angle through the cap into a leg.

6 The plywood base (F) is a piece of ½" exterior sheeting plywood. Drill holes for drainage. The board rests on the cleats. If necessary, this board can be easily changed. Finally, sand the planter and apply an exterior finish. I used Sikkens Cetol 1 #045 Mahogany.

CONSTRUCTION NOTES

- The height and width of this planter can be changed with a few simple calculations.
- I purchased ready-made cedar bead board, but you can make your own with a router and beading bit. Or you can make the panels thicker and install them directly into the leg grooves. If you have a router table, the plywood and panel can be made as one solid wood panel. The applied panel design I've shown is the simplest option.
- The square legs can be made round using dowel stock or a lathe. Cutting grooves in round stock is a little tricky and potentially dangerous, so make certain of the procedure and that the tools are properly equipped for safety.
- Any wood is suitable for this project, even soft pine as long as it's adequately protected with a good-quality finish. Cedar can be left natural, and it will soon turn a rustic gray. However, other woods that aren't so resistant will need a good weatherproof finish.

planter bench

This planter bench is great for the garden, patio or deck. It gives the gardener a place to display his or her favorite flowers and an opportunity to sit and admire them. It consists of two planters supporting a bench. The planter boxes, which serve as legs for the bench seat, are built using mortise-and-tenon joinery. The bench is a series of $1\frac{1}{2}$"-square boards secured to each planter with screws on the underside through the box rails. If possible, I always try to attach seat boards from the underside. Screw and nail heads can get very hot, and sitting on one in the summer, when we tend to wear lightweight clothing, isn't pleasant and can be dangerous. If you can't avoid using a screw on the top side of a seat, counterbore the hole and fill it with a wood plug.

I used cedar for this project, but any lumber, including pressure-treated wood, can be used.

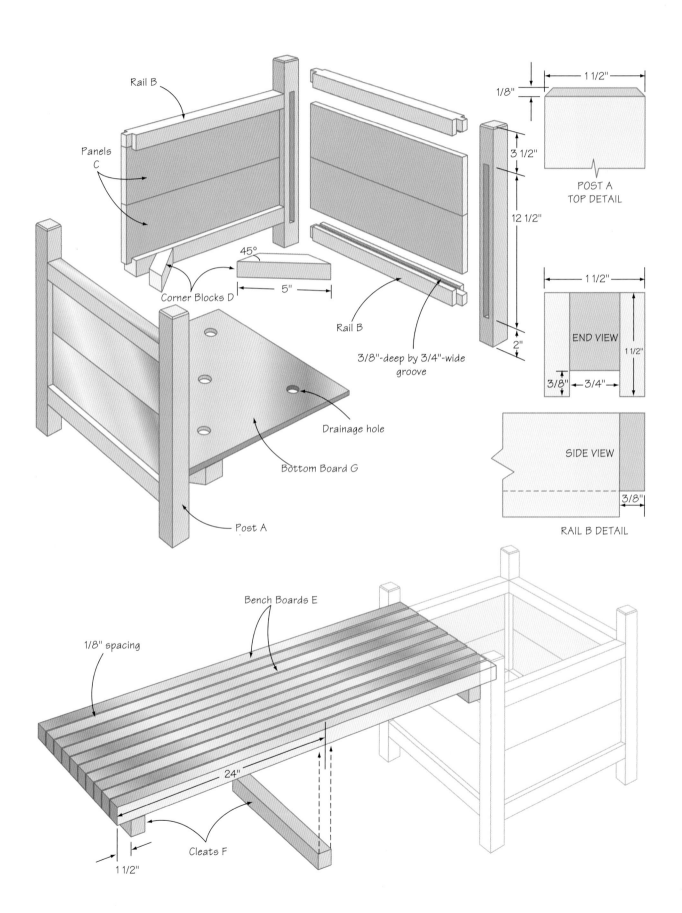

Rail B

Panels C

Corner Blocks D

45°

5"

Rail B

3/8"-deep by 3/4"-wide groove

Drainage hole

Bottom Board G

Post A

1/8"

1 1/2"

3 1/2"

12 1/2"

2"

POST A
TOP DETAIL

1 1/2"

END VIEW

1 1/2"

3/8"

3/4"

SIDE VIEW

3/8"

RAIL B DETAIL

Bench Boards E

1/8" spacing

24"

Cleats F

1 1/2"

CUTTING LIST • **planter bench**

REF.	QTY.	PART	MATERIAL	THICK	WIDTH	LENGTH	COMMENTS
A	8	Posts	Cedar	1½	1½	18	
B	16	Rails	Cedar	1½	1½	17¼	
C	16	Panels	Cedar	¾	5⅛	17¼	
D	8	Corner blocks	Cedar	1½	1½	5	Mitered
E	10	Bench boards	Cedar	1½	1½	48	
F	3	Cleats	Cedar	1½	1½	15½	
G	2	Bottom boards	Plywood	½	16¼	16¼	

Hardware and Supplies

2½" Exterior-rated wood screws

Polyurethane glue

Sikkens Cetol 1 #085 Teak finish

REQUIRED tools

Table Saw or Circular Saw

Drill

Jigsaw

Miter Box

Combination Square

Hammer

Screw Gun or Drivers

Sander or Sandpaper
and Block

Router and Bits

1 The eight posts (A) require two ¾"-wide by ⅜"-deep grooves that are 12½" long. Start the plunge cut on a router table 2" up from the bottom of each post. Mark the bottom with an "X" for reference. The grooves on each post are centered and on adjoining faces.

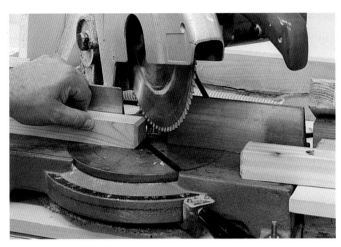

2 In a miter saw, or with a miter box, cut the corners off the top of each post at 45° to remove the sharp corners. Cut each corner approximately ⅛" from the top or the thickness of a blade.

3 Cut the 16 rails (B) and rout a groove in the center of one face on each post. The groove is ¾" wide by ⅜" deep. Form a tenon on both ends of each rail. The tenon is centered on the ends and is ¾" wide by ⅜" long by 1⅛" high. The first cut is the shoulder, which is made using the miter fence on a table saw. Set the blade ⅜" high and cut the notch ⅜" back from each end.

4 The cheek cuts are made with the saw blade ⅜" high. Set the fence 1¼" away from the blade and make the four cuts on each rail forming the tenons.

5 Cut the 16 panel boards (C). Each panel consists of two rails with the panels fitting into their grooves. Then assemble four panels, two from each planter, with polyurethane glue, and clamp.

Tip

I used a router bit to form my grooves in the posts. The tenons will have to be rounded over on the end opposite the groove so they will fit in the posts.

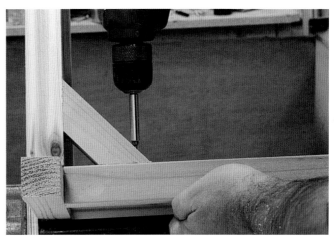

6 Join the two panel sets together with the remaining rails and panels to form the two planters. Apply glue to all the pieces and clamp securely.

7 Before the glue sets up, install four corner blocks (D) in each planter. Cut them on both ends with a 45° miter and attach them to the bottom rails with glue and screws. These blocks will square each planter and support a bottom board.

9 Secure the bench to the planters with screws through the cleats into a rail. Then as shown here, cut and install the two ½" × 16¼"-square exterior plywood bottom boards (G). The boards sit on top of the corner blocks. Drill a few holes in each for drainage, then sand and apply an exterior paint or stain. I used Sikkens Cetol 1 #085 Teak.

8 Cut the 10 bench boards (E) and sand smooth. Then prepare the three cleats (F) that will join the bench boards. Use a miter box to cut the corners off both ends on one face of each cleat. This will lessen the possibility of some-one hurting themselves on a sharp corner. Then as shown in the photo above, lay the bench boards upside down on a workbench, using spacers to hold the boards ⅛" apart. Attach one cleat in the center and the other two 1½" in from each end, using glue and 2½" exterior-rated screws.

CONSTRUCTION NOTES

- The bench can be made longer, but I wouldn't go over five feet. It's quite heavy and could damage the planter rails.
- If you want the bench a little higher, make the posts longer and begin the plunge cut for each groove farther up the post. I didn't glue my bench to the planter, so it can be dismantled and stored during the winter months.
- I used cedar for my planter bench, but any type of wood can be used as long as it is properly protected.

corner privacy screen

Privacy screens come in many shapes and sizes. Most of them simply block the view and serve no other purpose. This one is multifunctional. It can be anchored as a permanent fixture or be moved around. The seat offers a nice comfortable place to relax, and the lattice screen is perfect for that climbing vine you've always wanted to grow.

This project uses the new plastic lattice now available in home stores. It's a little more expensive, but it's maintenance-free and never needs painting. The cross-laps are a continuous mold, so the entire grid is one piece. It comes in 4' x 8' sheets and is available in a variety of colors and grid patterns. It can't be glued in place but is easily attached with screws through drilled holes.

I used cedar for my project with a cedar-colored lattice. But it would also look great using pressure-treated wood painted white with a matching lattice.

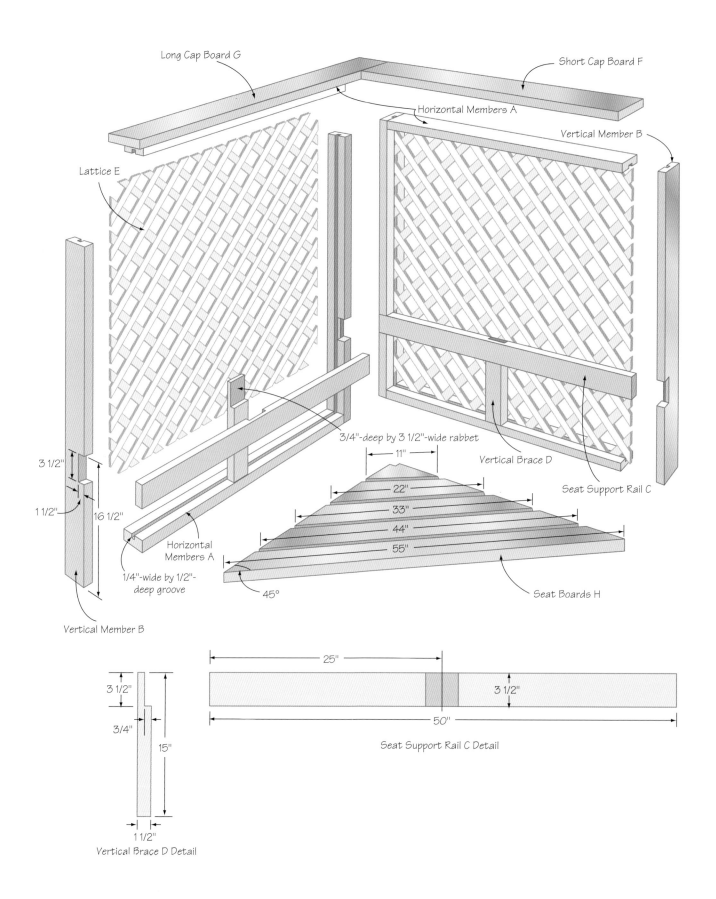

Long Cap Board G

Short Cap Board F

Horizontal Members A

Vertical Member B

Lattice E

3/4"-deep by 3 1/2"-wide rabbet

Vertical Brace D

Seat Support Rail C

3 1/2"

1 1/2"

16 1/2"

Horizontal Members A

1/4"-wide by 1/2"-deep groove

11"

22"

33"

44"

55"

45°

Seat Boards H

Vertical Member B

3 1/2"

3/4"

15"

1 1/2"

Vertical Brace D Detail

25"

3 1/2"

50"

Seat Support Rail C Detail

CUTTING LIST • **corner privacy screen**

REF.	QTY.	PART	MATERIAL	THICK	WIDTH	LENGTH	COMMENTS
A	4	Horizontal members	Cedar	$1\frac{1}{2}$	$3\frac{1}{2}$	47	
B	4	Vertical members	Cedar	$1\frac{1}{2}$	$3\frac{1}{2}$	50	
C	2	Seat support rails	Cedar	$1\frac{1}{2}$	$3\frac{1}{2}$	50	
D	2	Vertical braces	Cedar	$1\frac{1}{2}$	$3\frac{1}{2}$	15	
E	2	Lattices	Plastic	$\frac{1}{4}$	$47\frac{7}{8}$	$47\frac{7}{8}$	
F	1	Short cap board	Cedar	$\frac{3}{4}$	$5\frac{1}{2}$	50	
G	1	Long cap board	Cedar	$\frac{3}{4}$	$5\frac{1}{2}$	54	
H	5	Seat boards	Cedar	$1\frac{1}{2}$	$5\frac{1}{2}$	11, 22, 33, 44, & 55 long, mitered at 45°

Hardware and Supplies

3" Ceramic-coated exterior screws

$2\frac{1}{2}$" Ceramic-coated exterior screws

$1\frac{1}{4}$" Ceramic-coated exterior screws

Polyurethane glue or construction adhesive

Sikkens Cetol I #996 Natural Light finish

REQUIRED **tools**

Table Saw or Circular Saw

Drill

Combination Square

Hammer

Screw Gun or Drivers

Sander or Sandpaper
and Block

Router and Bits

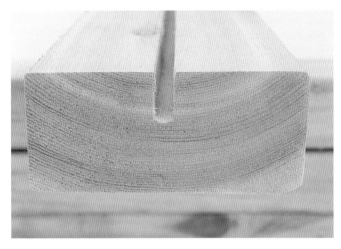

1 The four horizontal members (A) require a ¼"-wide by ½"-deep groove centered on one 3½" face of each board. The easiest way to cut the groove is with a table saw or ¼" bit in a router table.

2 Prepare the four vertical members (B) and cut a groove to match the horizontal frame pieces. One edge of each vertical member needs a 1½"-deep by 3½"-high notch to receive the seat supports. The top of each notch is 16½" from the bottom. Cut the notch with a table saw or jigsaw. Note that you will be creating a left and right upright. Verify that the notches face inward and the orientation to each other is correct for both pairs.

Plastic Lattice Tips

• The plastic lattice I purchased was ¼" thick. However, there may be differences between manufacturers' products, so buy it before you begin the project. If your lattice thickness is different from mine, adjust the cut of the groove on all horizontal and vertical frame members. Make a few test cuts until your lattice fits properly in the grooves.
• The lattice work height can be altered to suit your needs. This plastic lattice is available in 4' x 8' sheets and is easily cut with a jigsaw.
• When I was buying my plastic lattice I noticed that it was available in sheets with smaller holes. That will cut down on the breeze and light through the grid, but offer more privacy.

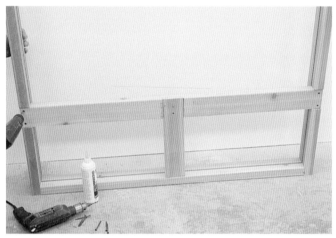

3 Cut a ¾"-deep by 3½"-wide dado centered on each seat support rail (C). Then for each of the two vertical braces (D) that attach between the seat support rails and the bottom horizontal members, cut a 3½"-high by ¾"-deep rabbet on one end. (The rabbet is cut on a 3½" face on both boards, and will fit into the dado on the seat support rail, forming a half-lap joint.) Then as shown here, begin the frame assembly by attaching two vertical members (B) to one horizontal member (A). Install the seat support rail (C) between the two verticals, and the vertical brace (D) to the seat rail. Do not install the top horizontal member now. Use an exterior-rated adhesive such as polyurethane glue or the construction type in a caulking gun. Drill pilot holes for the screws. Deck-type screws for outdoor use are required. I used 3" ceramic-coated exterior screws. Glue and secure the half-lap joint with 1¼"-long screws.

4 Slip the lattice pieces (E) into each frame. Install the top horizontal frame members and secure with glue and 2½" screws.

Tip

Always use a pilot hole when installing screws close to the end of any board. This good woodworking procedure ensures a stronger joint and often prevents wood splits.

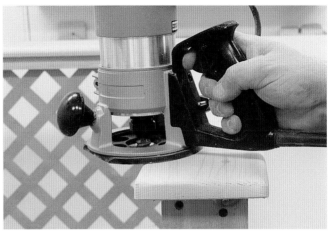

6 Using glue and 1¼" screws, install the cap boards (F and G) on top of the frames, aligning them so they hang over the top horizontal members by 1" on all edges. To prevent injuries lest someone bump into the frame, slightly ease the four outside corners of the cap boards using a belt sander. Then as shown here, use a ⅜" roundover bit in a router to dress the edges.

5 Further strengthen the lattice with three screws through it and into the seat support rail. Space them equally across the width of the rail. Then join the two frame sections together. Drive 2½" screws through the inside face of one vertical member and into the edge of the other panel's vertical member.

7 The first seat board (H) is 11" long, measured from the longest points of the two 45°-angle cuts on each end. It must be notched to fit around both frame vertical members. Drill pilot holes and secure the board with 2½" screws and glue. Drive the screws below the seat surface. Two screws per board will hold them securely.

CONSTRUCTION NOTES

- My project has five seat boards, but yours can have as many or as few as you like. If you eliminate the seat boards completely, screw the frame to a deck or secure it to the ground with stakes.
- If you want to build individual frame panels without the seat rails, cut 1"-deep grooves in your framework.
- Instead of plastic, this project can be built with cedar or pressure-treated lattice. In that event, use a 1"-deep groove and construction adhesive.
- Stain your entire project prior to installing the lattice. That way you won't have to worry about getting stain on the pre-colored lattice sections.

8 Install the remaining four seat boards, spacing them ⅛" apart. Each seat board dimension shown in the cutting list is from the longest point of the 45° miters on both ends of the boards. Finally, prepare the project for finishing by sanding all the wood members. Apply the finish of your choice. I used a stain called Sikkens Cetol 1 #996 Natural Light.

classic garden bench

This bench is an adaptation of the timeless styles found in many gardens. It has curved back legs and tapered front legs with a curved seat. It's a comfortable piece of furniture even without cushions.

Though many classic bench styles use mortise-and-tenon joinery, I designed this project with simpler butt joints, which depend more on new adhesives and weather-resistant hardware. It's a departure from the classic building style, but it's just as sturdy.

The back legs are a bit tricky, but are easily cut with a jigsaw once you've created a pattern. The only other challenges are the grooves on the upper and lower back rails. They can be made with a router or with a dado blade in your table saw. If you own a router table, the procedure is quick and easy. But remember they are deep cuts, so make a number of passes or you'll damage the bit or blade.

I made my bench with ash, but any wood is suitable as long as it's properly assembled and protected against the weather. Like all outdoor furniture, it will be exposed to sun, wind, damp and dry conditions, so make certain moisture isn't trapped where wood joins and the wood is properly finished.

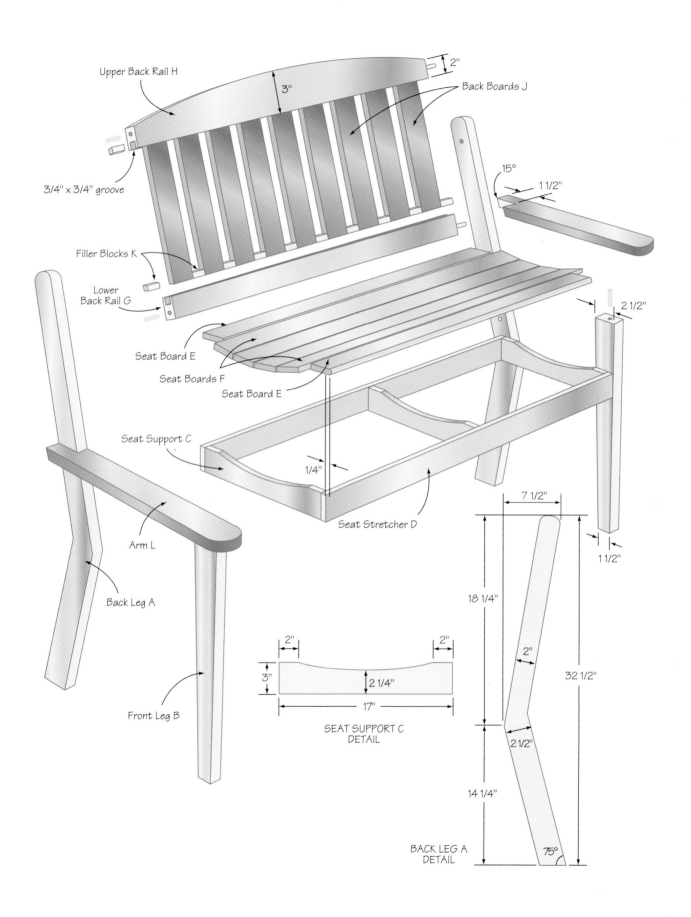

Upper Back Rail H

3"

2"

Back Boards J

3/4" x 3/4" groove

15°

1 1/2"

Filler Blocks K

Lower
Back Rail G

2 1/2"

Seat Board E

Seat Boards F

Seat Board E

1/4"

Seat Support C

Seat Stretcher D

7 1/2"

1 1/2"

Arm L

Back Leg A

18 1/4"

2"

Front Leg B

2"

2"

3"

2 1/4"

32 1/2"

17"

SEAT SUPPORT C
DETAIL

2 1/2"

14 1/4"

BACK LEG A
DETAIL

75°

CUTTING LIST • **classic garden bench**

REF.	QTY.	PART	MATERIAL	THICK	WIDTH	LENGTH	COMMENTS
A	2	Back legs	Ash	$1\frac{1}{2}$	$7\frac{1}{2}$	33	Cut as detailed
B	2	Front legs	Ash	$1\frac{1}{2}$	$2\frac{1}{2}$	$21\frac{1}{2}$	Taper cut
C	3	Seat supports	Ash	$1\frac{1}{2}$	3	17	
D	2	Seat stretchers	Ash	$\frac{3}{4}$	3	47	
E	2	Seat boards	Ash	$\frac{3}{4}$	3	47	
F	4	Seat boards	Ash	$\frac{3}{4}$	3	48	
G	1	Lower back rail	Ash	$1\frac{1}{2}$	2	47	
H	1	Upper back rail	Ash	$1\frac{1}{2}$	3	47	Curved
J	9	Back boards	Ash	$\frac{3}{4}$	3	13	
K	20	Filler blocks	Ash	$\frac{3}{4}$	$\frac{3}{4}$	2	
L	2	Arms	Ash	$1\frac{1}{2}$	3	23	

Hardware and Supplies

$\frac{1}{2}$" -dia. x 3" dowel pins

$\frac{1}{2}$"-dia. x $1\frac{7}{8}$" dowel pins

$2\frac{1}{2}$" Ceramic-coated exterior screws

2" Ceramic-coated exterior screws

Finishing nails

Wood plugs

Polyurethane glue

Sikkens Cetol 1 #996 Natural Light Finish

REQUIRED tools

Table Saw or Circular Saw

Drill

Jigsaw or Band Saw

Combination Square

Hammer

Screw Gun or Drivers

Sander or Sandpaper and Block

Router and Bits

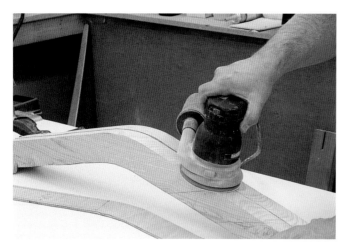

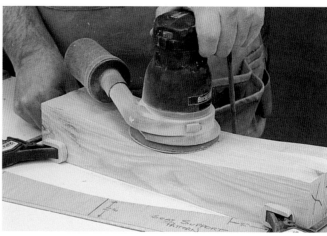

1 Create a back leg pattern using the drawing as a guide. Cut the legs (A) from 2×8 stock and clamp them together when finish-sanding to ensure they are identical.

2 Create a pattern for the two front tapered legs (B), and cut them out with either a jigsaw, band saw, or on a table saw if you have a tapering jig. Once again, clamp the rough-cut pieces together and sand them so they are smooth and identical. Then with a ⅜" roundover bit, ease all the edges. Don't round over the top or bottom ends of the front legs or the bottoms on the back legs. However, the round tops on the back legs should be eased with the router bit. Next, make a pattern for the three seat supports (C) and cut them to size. Then as shown here, clamp all three together and sand so the curve is equal on all the supports.

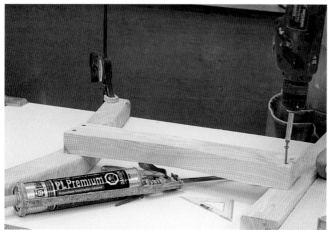

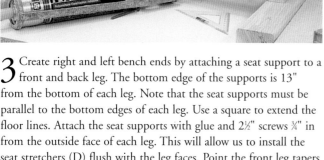

3 Create right and left bench ends by attaching a seat support to a front and back leg. The bottom edge of the supports is 13" from the bottom of each leg. Note that the seat supports must be parallel to the bottom edges of each leg. Use a square to extend the floor lines. Attach the seat supports with glue and 2½" screws ¾" in from the outside face of each leg. This will allow us to install the seat stretchers (D) flush with the leg faces. Point the front leg tapers to the inside or toward the back legs.

4 Use an assembled end to align the second end to ensure both are identical. Attach the seat supports with polyurethane glue and 2½" screws.

Tip

The simplest way to ensure the bench ends are assembled correctly is to clamp each front and back leg tightly on a flat surface. Draw a reference line representing the floor on your workbench and align the legs.

6 Secure the third seat support at the center of the seat stretchers. Once again, use glue and screws in counterbored holes that can be filled with wood plugs.

5 Attach the front and rear seat stretchers (D) with two 2½" screws in counterbored holes. Use wood plugs to fill the holes.

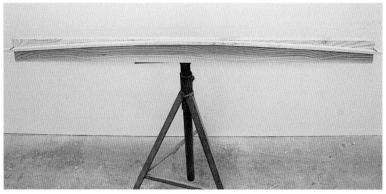

7 Begin attaching the seat boards (E) with glue and screws in counterbored holes. One screw at each seat support will be adequate. The shorter seat boards will be used as the first and last slats. Round over one upper and lower edge on a short seat board using a ⅜" roundover bit in a router. This will be the front edge of the first slat. It should be installed so it extends past the front face of the seat stretcher by ¼". Install the remaining slats, spacing them ³⁄₁₆" apart.

8 Cut both back rails (G and H). The lower rail (G) is a simple straight cut, and the upper piece (H) requires an arched top. A bow jig can be used to draw the arch. The bow jig is made by cutting a ¼"-thick strip of wood that's ¾" wide by 50" long. Drive finishing nails into the upper rail ⅛" from each end and 1" from the top edge. Drive a third nail at the center of the rail ⅛" from the top edge. Bend the wood so it's in front of the end nails and behind the center nail. Draw the arc behind the bow and cut along the line.

Tip

The seat boards may be uneven from board to board. Their position is dependent on how the seat support curve was cut. After securing all the boards, use a sander to smooth out any differences in level from board to board. Normally, the variations are small and can easily be removed with sandpaper.

9 Sand both rails and use a ⅜" roundover bit to soften the edges. Don't round over the ends. Then cut a ¾"-wide by ¾"-deep groove centered on the top of the bottom rail and bottom edge of the top rail. The cut can be made with a router table or table saw. But don't try to make the groove in one pass — it's a lot of wood to remove, and multiple passes are the safest method of removal.

10 Prepare to assemble the back by cutting the nine back boards (J) and 20 filler blocks (K). Each back board is spaced with a filler block in the upper and lower rails. Begin the assembly with filler blocks, using glue. Clamp the back when fully assembled and set it aside to cure.

12 Rough-cut the arms (L) to size. Then, hold each one in its proper position and make the angle cuts for the front and back edges of the leg. Use a level to ensure the arm is correctly positioned before marking.

Tip

You can make dowel pin installation easier by slightly tapering the dowel end that will be inserted into the hole. Lightly round the end with a belt sander or a sanding block.

11 Clamp the back assembly between the two rear legs. The back is positioned ⅜" above the seat boards and centered on each leg. Drill four ½"-diameter holes 3" deep through each leg and into the ends of the lower and upper back rails. Use polyurethane glue on four ½"-diameter by 3"-long pieces of dowel rod. After making certain the holes are well coated with adhesive, drive the dowel rods flush with each leg face. Leave the back clamped until the adhesive cures.

13 Test-fit the arm after cutting a notch, and sand if necessary.

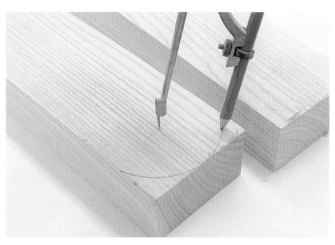

14 Round the fronts of each arm by cutting a 1½"-radius arc. Use a jigsaw or band saw to make the cuts, then sand the arm smooth.

15 After verifying that the arms fit and completing the sanding, round over the top and bottom edges with a ⅜" router bit. Do not round the edges of the notches. Then as shown here, clamp the arms in place and draw the perimeter outline of the front leg end on the underside of each arm.

CONSTRUCTION NOTES

- Remember to plug all the counterbored holes with wood plugs. If you don't plan to fill these holes, don't counterbore the screws. That open hole will allow moisture and dirt to build up and start wood rot.
- If you're having difficulty holding the filler blocks in place, pin them with a galvanized brad nail from the rear side of the rails.
- Don't forget to apply a good coat of finish to all the exposed surfaces.

16 Drill a ½"-diameter by 1"-deep hole in the center of both front leg ends and the center of the outline on the underside of each arm. Next, cut two hardwood dowels ½" in diameter by 1⅞" long. Attach the arms to the front leg ends, using the dowels and an adhesive. Attach the back end of the arms to each rear leg, using glue and two 2" screws in counterbored holes. Fill the holes with wood plugs. Finally, sand the bench to prepare it for finishing. Use a good-quality exterior finish. I chose Sikkens Cetol 1 #996 Natural Light for my bench.

curved planter bench

This planter bench is a popular garden accent and is an expensive piece of outdoor furniture if purchased at a store. However, the cost is due to the amount of time required to build it, not to the materials. So you'll save quite a few dollars constructing it yourself. Plus this project allows you to combine two favorite summer pastimes — relaxing and looking at flowers. What more could you ask for?

My planter bench features a curved container for flowers and a curved bench support. It's a bit challenging but, like many woodworking projects, much simpler than it first appears. It's built from construction-grade cedar. And, as with any other garden structure, I've used exterior-rated adhesives and fasteners. A great deal of nailing is necessary, so be sure to use galvanized finishing nails.

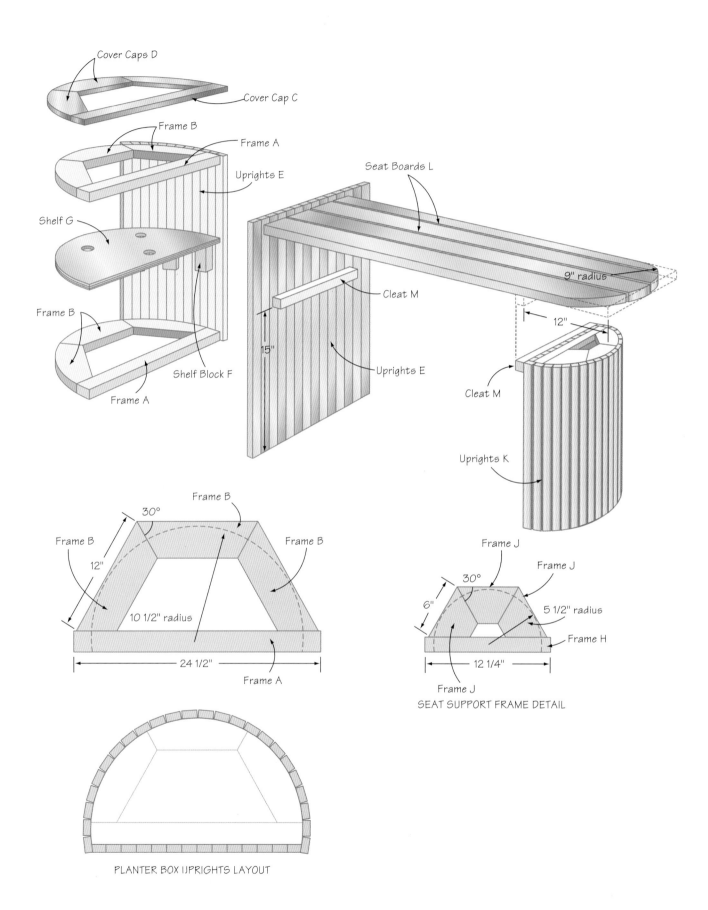

Cover Caps D

Cover Cap C

Frame B

Frame A

Uprights E

Seat Boards L

Shelf G

9" radius

Cleat M

Frame B

15"

12"

Shelf Block F

Uprights E

Frame A

Cleat M

Uprights K

Frame B

30°

Frame B

Frame B

Frame J

Frame J

12"

6"

30°

10 1/2" radius

5 1/2" radius

Frame H

24 1/2"

12 1/4"

Frame A

Frame J

SEAT SUPPORT FRAME DETAIL

PLANTER BOX UPRIGHTS LAYOUT

CUTTING LIST • **curved planter bench**

REF.	QTY.	PART	MATERIAL	THICK	WIDTH	LENGTH	COMMENTS
Planter Box							
A	2	Frame members	Cedar	1½	2	24½	
B	6	Frame members	Cedar	1½	3½	12	Angled 30°
C	1	Cover cap	Cedar	¾	2½	26	
D	3	Cover caps	Cedar	¾	4¼	13	Angled 30°
E	38	Uprights	Cedar	¾	1½	24	
F	6	Shelf blocks	Cedar	¾	1½	4	
G	1	Shelf	Plywood	½	10½		Radius measurement
Seat Support							
H	2	Frame members	Cedar	1½	1½	12¼	
J	6	Frame members	Cedar	1½	3½	6	Angled 30°
K	30	Uprights	Cedar	¾	1	16½	
Seat							
L	4	Seat boards	Cedar	1½	3½	47	
M	2	Cleats	Cedar	1½	1½	14	

Hardware and Supplies

Polyurethane glue

3" Exterior-rated screws

2½" Exterior-rated screws

2" Exterior-rated screws

Galvanized finishing nails

Sikkens Cetol 1 #078 Natural finish

REQUIRED **tools**

Table Saw or Circular Saw

Drill

Jigsaw or Band Saw

Combination Square

Hammer

Screw Gun or Drivers

Sander or Sandpaper and Block

Nail Set

1 Prepare all the parts for the planter frames. The frame members (A) are straight cuts. However, the angled frame members B are all cut at 30°. The lengths of all B pieces are measured between the longest angle points. Cut the frame members (A and B), then brush on an even coat of glue and secure each joint of the upper and lower planter frames with 3" screws. The screws act as clamps and hold the joint securely until the glue cures. Remove the screws before cutting the half-circles.

2 After the adhesive cures, find the center of frame member A and draw a 10½"-radius half-circle. Cut along each line with a jigsaw. Don't forget to remove any screws that are in the way.

3 A cover cap is required for the top frame. Cut all the C and D pieces, with the D pieces at 30°. Attach them to one frame member with glue and screws. Align the inside edge of cover cap C flush with the inside edge of the frame's base and let the overlap extend equally on the other edges.

4 Attach the remaining cap members (D). Now, draw an 11¼" radius from the center of board C, 1¼" up from the bottom edge. The arc should be ¾" wider than the frame arc on all edges. Check the lines before you cut the cap, and adjust if necessary.

Tip

If you don't have a large compass, make a "stick" compass with a flat board, a nail and a pencil. Or use a piece of string to draw the arc.

5 Glue and nail 24 uprights (E) around the circumference of the upper and lower frames. The "first" and "last" uprights should be attached first, and should overlap the straight edges of the frame by ¾". That overlap will cover the edges of the back uprights. Don't install the 14 back uprights (E) at this time.

Tip

Be sure to attach the "first" and "last" uprights first, before filling in the space between them. This will give the "first" and "last" uprights an equal ¾" overlap. If the interior uprights don't fill the space evenly, the sizes can be altered slightly to make them fit. It may rquire the last four or five uprights to be cut to fit.

6 The six shelf blocks (F) are attached to the inside of the planter uprights. The height depends on the type of plant you use. Use glue and nails, spacing five blocks around the inside circumference of the circle. The sixth block will be installed on the inside center of the back uprights.

7 Cut the half-circle shelf (G) from exterior plywood sheeting. It sits on the shelf support blocks. Drill a few holes for water drainage.

Tip

You will probably have to slightly adjust the width of the last few uprights. This is due to small circumference differences that, over such a large arc, do occur. And when you are nearing the end, dry fit the last four or five uprights and trim if necessary. Each upright should butt tightly against the one beside it on the back faces.

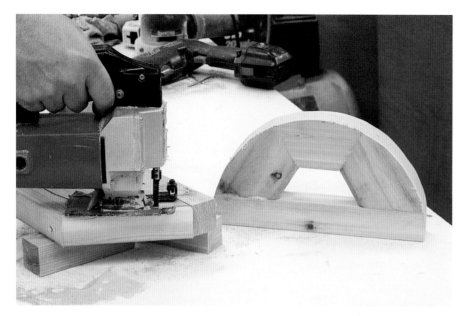

8 Attach the 14 remaining back uprights (E). Remember to install the final shelf block (F) on the center upright. The seat support frame is constructed following the same procedures as the planter box frame. However, it's smaller in diameter and doesn't need a cover cap. Cut the frame members (H and J). Build the upper and lower frames. Then as shown here, draw a 5½"-radius half-circle on both and cut with a jigsaw.

9 Cut the 30 seat support uprights (K) using glue and nails, and install all but the back ones at this time.

10 The seat is made with four boards and two cleats. Attach one of the cleats (M) to the bottom side of the seat boards (L) so it's flush at one end. Use glue and 2½" screws. Use spacers to hold the seat boards in place with ⅛" gap between them.

11 Attach the second cleat 12" back from the opposite end. Then draw a 9" arc on that end of the seat, and as shown here, cut the arc with a jigsaw and sand smooth.

12 Attach two of the remaining uprights (K) on the back side of the seat support — one at each end. Turn the bench seat upside down and attach the seat support, tightly against the cleat, with glue and screws. Drive three 2½" screws into the seat boards through the upper seat support frame.

13 Install the remaining uprights (K) on the seat support back. Then attach the seat-and-support assembly to the planter box using glue and five 2" screws spaced evenly across the cleat. The top of the bench is 18" above the ground and centered on the planter back. Attach the units together by screwing through the cleat into the planter uprights. Finally, sand and apply a good exterior finish. I used Sikkens Cetol 1 #078 Natural for my project.

Angle-Cutting Secrets

You can accent the spaces between the uprights by angle-cutting their faces, or eliminate the spacing entirely by angle-cutting their backs. But how do you know the proper cutting angle? Here's a rough rule of thumb for uprights on a round surface.

First, the distance around a circle is found by multiplying 6.2832 by the radius. In this case the radius is 10½", so the distance or circumference is about 66". To completely surround the circle I would divide the upright width of 1½" into the circumference. I would therefore need about 44 pieces.

To find the angle of each one if I want to eliminate any space between them, I would divide the number of pieces (in this case, 44) into 360 (the total number of degrees in a circle), which would yield an angle of slightly greater than 8°. Since two uprights join to make the 8° angle, each one would be cut at about 4° (or half the angle).

All the calculations are close, but factors like upright thickness increase the circle circumference at the face. However, it will allow you to make a first test cut. It should be very close with only one or two slight adjustments required to accurately set your saw blade angle for all the uprights.

folding side table

Having a few extra side tables for your outdoor gatherings is a real benefit. But storing them can be time consuming, and they do take up a lot of space. This folding side table might be the answer. It's easy to store when not needed and rugged enough to be used outside.

I used birch for my tables because birch will take a lot of abuse. The dowels are maple, so having the two hardwoods pivot on each other isn't a problem. And they're both very close in color and grain structure, so the stain will tone equally.

This project should give you many years of service. Hardware has been kept to a minimum, and all the movable parts are wood, which lessens the chance of a mechanical failure. And the tabletop boards are spaced to provide drainage if you happen to leave the table out in the rain.

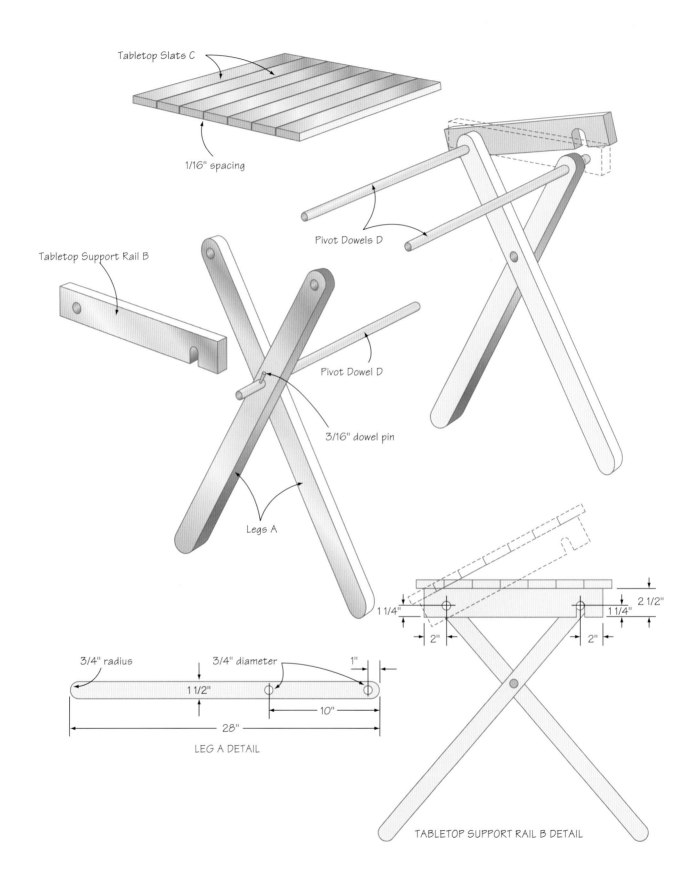

Tabletop Slats C

1/16" spacing

Pivot Dowels D

Tabletop Support Rail B

Pivot Dowel D

3/16" dowel pin

Legs A

3/4" radius

3/4" diameter

1"

1 1/2"

10"

28"

LEG A DETAIL

1 1/4"

2 1/2"

1 1/4"

2"

2"

TABLETOP SUPPORT RAIL B DETAIL

CUTTING LIST • folding side table

REF.	QTY.	PART	MATERIAL	THICK	WIDTH	LENGTH	COMMENTS
A	4	Legs	Birch	³/₄	1¹/₂	28	
B	2	Tabletop support rails	Birch	³/₄	2¹/₂	16	
C	7	Tabletop slats	Birch	³/₄	2¹/₂	16	
D	3	Pivot dowels	Maple	³/₄ dia.		14	

Hardware and Supplies

6" of ³/₁₆"-dia. dowel pin

1¹/₂" Exterior-rated screws

Wood plugs

Polyurethane glue

Sikkens Cetol 1 #072 Butternut finish

REQUIRED tools

Table Saw or Circular Saw

Drill

Combination Square

Hammer

Screw Gun or Drivers

Sander or Sandpaper
and Block

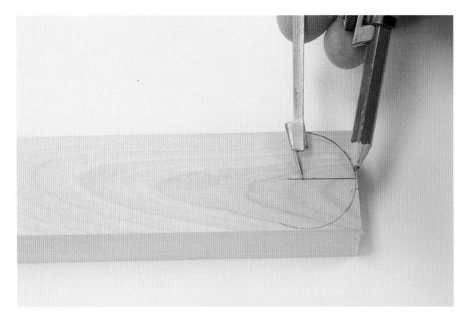

1 Draw a ¾"-radius arc on both ends of each leg (A). Rough-cut the arc with a jigsaw and sand smooth.

Tip

After rough-sanding the arc on all the legs, clamp them together and finish-sand all four. All legs will then be identical.

2 Drill two ¾"-diameter holes centered on each leg. The center of the first hole is 1" from the top, and the second hole is located 10" from the top. Then cut the two tabletop support rails (B) and sand smooth. Drill a ¾"-diameter hole 2" on center from each end on both rails. Center both holes on the rail face. Extend the diameter of one hole on each rail to the end to make a slot. Cut along the lines with a jigsaw and, as shown here, smooth the slot with sandpaper.

3 The seven tabletop slats (C) are attached to the two rails with exterior adhesive and 1½" screws. Install them with a ¹⁄₁₆" space in counterbored pilot holes. The tabletop slats extend 1" past the support rails on each side. Fill all the holes with wood plugs and sand smooth. Notice also that I eased the four outside corners by cutting a small miter in each.

Tip

Use a smaller-diameter dowel wrapped with sandpaper to smooth the slots. Note that the dowel material available in your area may be smaller or larger than what is stated. The ³⁄₄"-diameter dowel I purchased was actually ²³⁄₃₂".

4 Begin attaching the legs to the top assembly. Use one of the 14" pivot dowels (D). Push the pivot dowel through the slot of one tabletop support rail and slip on two legs. Then push the pivot dowel through the slot of the opposite tabletop support rail. Position each leg ⅟₁₆" away from the table supports. Drill a ³⁄₁₆"-diameter hole through the leg into the center of each pivot dowel and on through the other side. Drive a piece of ³⁄₁₆"-diameter dowel pin into the hole, pinning the leg. Put glue on the pin before driving it in, but be careful not to get any glue on the pivot dowel and the table support slot, as it must swing freely. Cut the dowel pin flush after it has been driven all the way in.

5 The center pivot also needs a 14" pivot rod (D). The center pivot dowel is aligned correctly when both ends are flush with the outside of the tabletop support rails. Dry fit the parts, then when everything is aligned, drill and install ³⁄₁₆"-diameter dowel pins through the pivot dowel on both sides of the two legs. Drill the hole ½" deep and leave ½" of dowel pin sticking out of each hole. Use glue on the pins but be careful, as the legs must move freely.

6 The remaining 14" pivot dowel is installed through the lower leg holes. Extend the pivot dowel 1½" past the outside face of each leg. Pin the legs to the pivot dowel. Finally, sand and apply a finish to your table. I used Sikkens Cetol 1 #072 Butternut.

CONSTRUCTION NOTES

- The height of this table can be altered to suit your specific needs. Simply vary the leg length and adjust the center holes accordingly.
- Instead of using wood dowel pins, you can use screws. I have tried to eliminate as much hardware as possible to keep that all-wood look, but it's a personal choice. Using a screw to pin the joints without glue means that you'll be able to take the table apart. That might be a desirable feature for you.
- Any hardwood is suitable for this table. Interchanging colors of table slats by using mahogany and birch or maple would be a nice design. An all-dark-wood top with light-colored legs is another option. However, that effect could be achieved with stain.
- This could also be used as a barbecue side table. Add 1½"-high rails to the top to keep anything from rolling off the table. It would also be handy for all the necessary spices and sauces needed when cooking outdoors. And when you're finished cooking, it could be used as a serving table.

outdoor coffee table

Though this coffee table is plain and the construction simple, it will look terrific on any deck or patio. I built mine with construction-grade cedar. I picked through the 1x4 material at my local lumberyard to find the best boards.

The joinery is basic, with the exception of the 45° angled rips on the legs. However, any size table saw can easily accomplish these cuts. The leg taper can be cut on a table saw, jigsaw or band saw. Use the one you feel most comfortable with to make these cuts. If the cuts are a little rough, sanding will straighten them out.

The large table surface is supported by four cross supports. Because I always prefer hiding fasteners, I drove the screws from under the table into the tabletop boards, which are spaced $1/16$" apart to provide drainage. I then hid the end grain of the tabletop boards by attaching a skirt around the table perimeter.

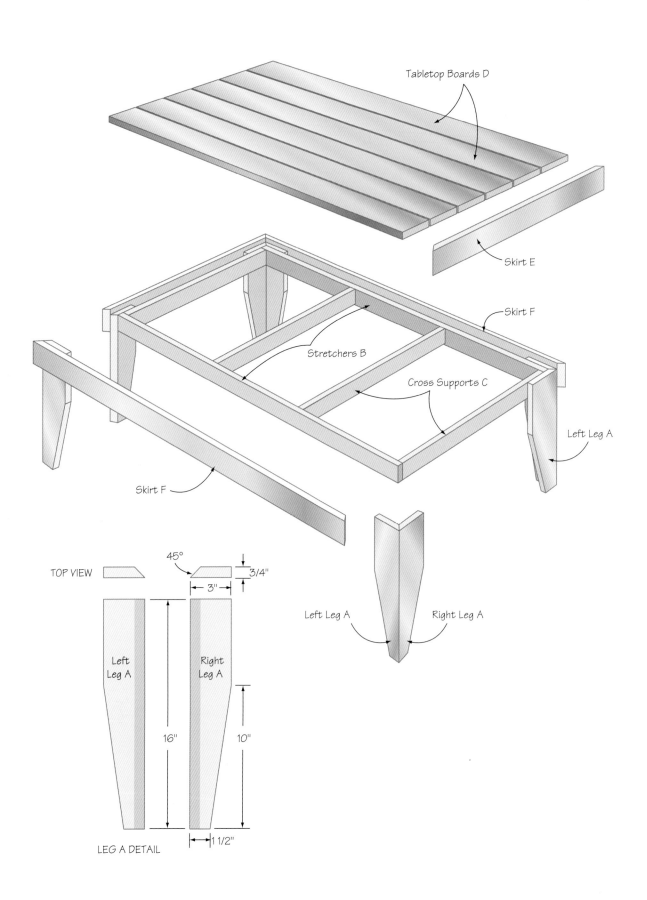

Tabletop Boards D

Skirt E

Skirt F

Stretchers B

Cross Supports C

Left Leg A

Skirt F

Left Leg A

Right Leg A

TOP VIEW

45°

3/4"

3"

Left
Leg A

Right
Leg A

16"

10"

1 1/2"

LEG A DETAIL

CUTTING LIST • **outdoor coffee table**

REF.	QTY.	PART	MATERIAL	THICK	WIDTH	LENGTH	COMMENTS
A	8	Legs	Cedar	$3/4$	3	16	Tapered and angle-cut
B	2	Stretchers	Cedar	$3/4$	$1^1/2$	36	
C	4	Cross supports	Cedar	$3/4$	$1^1/2$	18	
D	6	Tabletop boards	Cedar	$3/4$	$3^7/16$	$37^1/2$	
E	2	Skirt boards	Cedar	$3/4$	3	$22^1/2$	Mitered
F	2	Skirt boards	Cedar	$3/4$	3	39	Mitered

Hardware and Supplies

Polyurethane glue

$1^1/4$" Exterior-rated screws

2" Exterior-rated screws

Brad nails

Sikkens Cetol 1 #045 Mahogany finish

REQUIRED tools

Table Saw or Circular Saw

Drill

Miter Box

Combination Square

Hammer

Screw Gun or Drivers

Sander or Sandpaper and Block

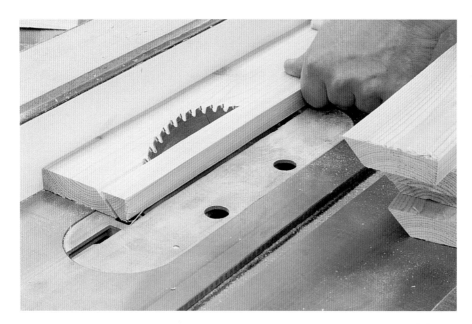

1 Prepare the eight legs (A) by ripping a 45° miter on one edge. The 3"-width dimension given is measured on the widest face.

2 Taper each leg on the edge opposite the 45° cut. Begin the taper at the bottom of each leg 1½" from the edge to a point 10" up from the bottom. Use a jigsaw or band saw to complete the cut. Remember that each leg set has a right and a left half, so be careful when laying out the tapers. Clamp all the legs together and sand the taper so they are all identical. Then as shown here, join the pairs of legs using polyurethane adhesive or any other exterior-rated glue. Keep them in alignment with brad nails and clamp the pairs together. There should be four identical leg assemblies.

3 Attach the stretchers (B) and two of the cross supports (C) to the four legs. Install them on the inside of each leg using glue and 1¼" screws. Verify that the overall dimension, measured on the outside faces of the legs, is 21" wide by 37½" long.

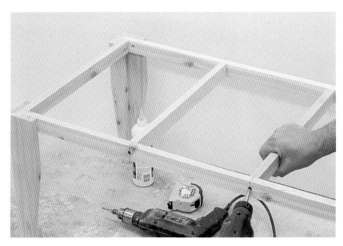

4 Glue and screw the two remaining cross supports (C) between the inside faces of the two stretchers (B). Divide the space equally into thirds and secure the supports.

5 Attach the tabletop boards (D) with glue and 2" screws in piloted holes through the cross supports. Space the boards ¹⁄₁₆" apart. The first and last boards should be flush with the outside leg faces. Before you begin securing the boards, dry fit the pieces. If the last board doesn't fit correctly, adjust all the gaps between the boards until a correct fit is achieved.

CONSTRUCTION NOTES

- The size of this table is easily changed because of its simple design. Altering the length and width is a straightforward procedure. After all, you might want a square coffee table instead of this rectangular design.

- If you have the room on your patio or deck, you could make a coffee table and two end tables, which are usually square and a little higher.

- This design can also be used to make a dining table. They are normally 30" high to the tabletop surface and 28" wide by 60" long. The only change I'd make with this larger table would be to increase the stretcher and cross supports widths to 3". It might also be worthwhile using a router and roundover bit to soften the top outside edge of the skirt boards.

- Just about any wood can be used to build this project. Softwoods or hardwoods work equally well; however, the harder species will tend to be a little stronger and heavier. But any wood that's properly protected will give you many years of service.

- The gaps between tabletop boards allow water to drain. If you plan to use this table in a closed sunroom or on a covered deck, the board width can be adjusted to eliminate the spaces.

6 The skirt is made with four boards (E and F), mitered at 45°. Apply glue and use 2" screws through the legs to secure the skirt. The skirt can also be nailed into the edge of the tabletop boards along its length. Finally, sand and apply a finish to your project. I used a stain called Sikkens Cetol 1 #045 Mahogany.

Tip

Always drill a pilot hole before securing with screws. This is especially important in thin stock and in end grain, but it should be a standard practice in any situation.

formal side table

If your backyard, patio or deck furniture style is formal, this side table will fit in perfectly. It is a little challenging, but take it one step at a time and you'll have no trouble at all.

The main feature of this project is the curved legs, which are cut from wide stock with a jigsaw or band saw. The other unique feature is the "breadboard" ends. The tabletop boards require tenons, and they fit into end boards that have a slot. The end grain on each board is hidden, which is always a benefit on any piece of outdoor furniture.

I've included a lower shelf on this table to both improve the look and add strength. It fits into notches cut in each of the legs, which are attached to the tabletop with dowels and glue.

Though I built my table with birch, just about any wood can be used. Hardwoods are a good choice because they add a lot of strength and will machine easily when using joints such as the mortise and tenon.

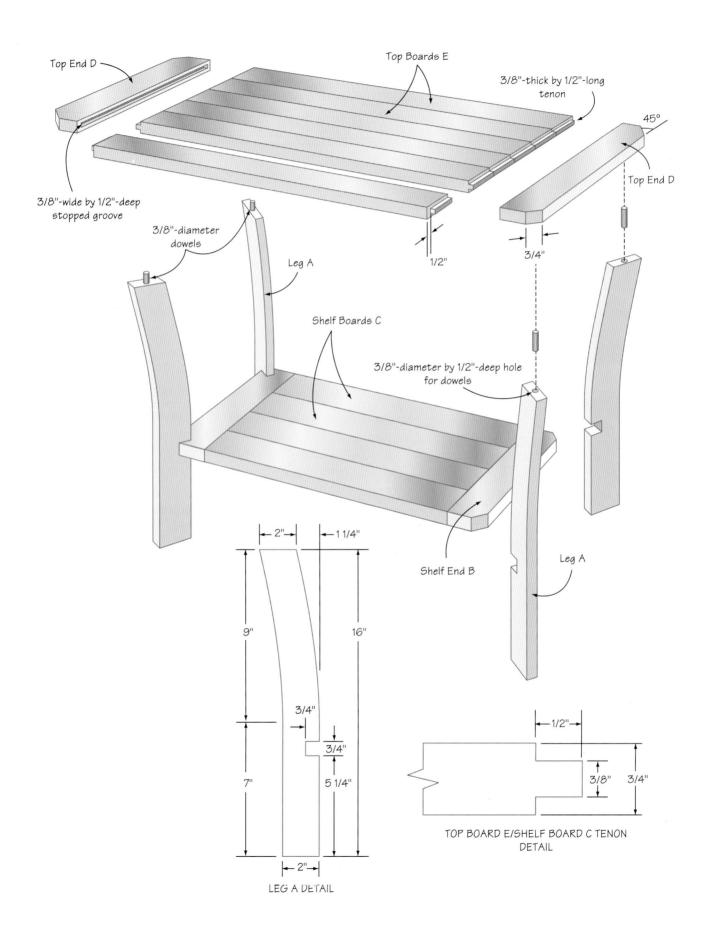

Top End D

Top Boards E

3/8"-thick by 1/2"-long tenon

45°

Top End D

3/8"-wide by 1/2"-deep stopped groove

1/2"

3/4"

3/8"-diameter dowels

Leg A

Shelf Boards C

3/8"-diameter by 1/2"-deep hole for dowels

3/8"-diameter by 1/2"-deep hole for dowels

Shelf End B

Leg A

2"

1 1/4"

9"

16"

3/4"

3/4"

7"

5 1/4"

2"

LEG A DETAIL

1/2"

3/8"

3/4"

TOP BOARD E/SHELF BOARD C TENON DETAIL

CUTTING LIST • **formal side table**

REF.	QTY.	PART	MATERIAL	THICK	WIDTH	LENGTH	COMMENTS
A	4	Legs	Birch	3/4	3 1/2	16	
B	2	Shelf ends	Birch	3/4	2 1/2	12	
C	4	Shelf boards	Birch	3/4	2 15/16	16	
D	2	Top ends	Birch	3/4	2 1/2	18	
E	6	Top boards	Birch	3/4	2 15/16	21	

Hardware and Supplies

1/4" Plywood for master leg pattern

3/8"-dia. x 7/8" dowels (for securing legs to tabletop)

1 1/2" Exterior-rated screws

Polyurethane glue

Sikkens Cetol 1 #009 Dark Oak finish

REQUIRED **tools**

Table Saw or Circular Saw

Drill

Jigsaw or Band Saw

Combination Square

Hammer

Screw Gun or Drivers

Sander or Sandpaper
and Block

Router and Bits

Clamps

1 Cut the four legs (A) from the rough-cut stock shown in the cutting list. See the drawing for exact dimensions. Use a jigsaw or band saw to cut the legs. Then as shown here, clamp the four legs together and sand smooth. Using this technique means that all legs will be identical.

2 Round over the four side edges of all legs. Use sandpaper or a ¼" roundover bit in a router table.

Tip

Make a master leg pattern using ¼" plywood. Using a pattern guarantees that all pieces will be identical. Many woodworkers keep the patterns for future projects. They are a real time-saver when you need another piece, particularly if you plan to make another similar project.

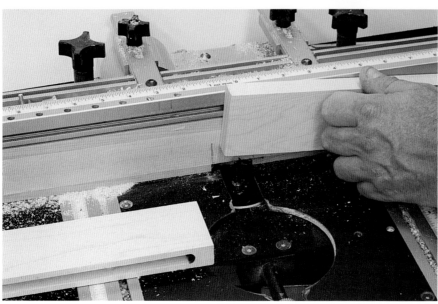

3 Cut the shelf breadboard ends (B). One edge of each board requires a stopped groove ⅜" wide by ½" deep. A stopped groove does not continue through each end of the board. It begins and ends ½" from the ends of each board. This type of cut is easily accomplished by plunging and lifting the workpiece on a router table. Draw guide marks on the table fence so that your board is properly positioned.

Tip

Cutting a deep groove on the breadboard ends puts a great deal of stress on a router bit. To achieve a better cut and prevent damage to the bit, make the groove in four or five passes.

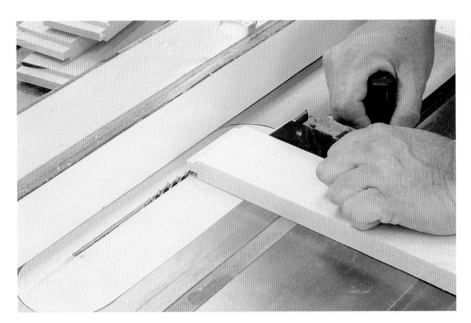

4 Each shelf board (C) needs a ⅜"-thick by ½"-long tenon on both ends. Form the tenon on a router table or table saw, but take the extra time to make certain it's centered on the board.

5 The two outside boards on the shelf must have their tenons cut back by ½" on the outward side. This is necessary because the breadboard ends have stopped grooves. You are creating a shoulder tenon, which will allow the board's outside edge to be aligned with the breadboard end. Because I used a router bit to cut the groove, I will have to round over the tenon on its outside edge.

6 Assemble the bottom shelf with exterior-rated polyurethane glue. Leave ⅛" spacing between the boards and clamp until the adhesive cures.

7 Sand the shelf. Then, cut each corner at 45° leaving a ¾"-wide face on the cut. The cut line is approximately ⅜" in from each corner. Ease the top and bottom edges using a ⅜" roundover bit in a router. But don't round the mitered corners.

8 Notch each leg 5¼" up from the bottom. The notch is ¾" high by ¾" deep. Use a table saw to quickly and accurately form the notches.

9 Install one leg at each mitered corner of the shelf. Drill and counterbore a pilot hole at an angle through the bottom of the shelf into each leg. Use glue and a 1½"-long screw to secure each leg.

10 Construct the top following the same procedures as the shelf. However, it's larger with a finished size of 18" deep by 25" wide. Cut the stopped grooves in the breadboard ends, form the tenons, and reduce the outside tenons. Do not miter the corners; use a belt sander to round them over. Sand and round over the top and bottom edge. Turn the completed top upside down on the workbench. Place the legs, with attached shelf, on the top. Position the legs with equal spacing on all four edges of the tabletop. Then as shown here, use a pencil to trace around the perimeter of each leg.

11 Mark a point 1" in from the outside edge of each leg. Center this mark on the leg end. Mark the tabletop leg pattern the same way. Now, drill a ⅜" hole ½" deep in the table and another ⅜" hole in the leg.

Tip

Whenever you're locating and marking the final position of an assembly, use witness marks. These are pencil markings that allow you to return the assembly to its original position.

CONSTRUCTION NOTES

- I used a hardwood for this project because I didn't feel comfortable with softwood. Four notches support the bottom shelf, so the wood has to span between legs without any other support.
- You can alter the size by changing dimensions on the bottom shelf and tabletop. Leg length can be changed if you want to make a matching coffee table. Two end tables with a matching coffee table would be a stunning addition to any outdoor setting.
- There are many hardwoods and all would be suitable to build this table. And if you plan to use this project in a sheltered place, you can lessen or eliminate the spacing between shelf and tabletop boards.
- Different wood types would also be real eye pleasers. Use one species for the breadboard ends and another for the field boards.
- And finally, don't forget to file those ¼" patterns in a safe place. They might be useful in the future.

12 Drive ⅜"-diameter dowels in the tabletop using polyurethane glue. Put a little glue in each leg hole and tap the leg assembly onto the four dowels. Finally, sand the table and apply an outdoor finish. I used Sikkens Cetol 1 #009 Dark Oak.

tête-à-tête bench

This bench will be a great addition to any outdoor setting. And, best of all, it's easy to build. I used construction-grade cedar for this project, but any number of wood species, such as pine, spruce, pressure-treated, or some of the hardwoods like ash or oak, would be suitable.

This loop-leg design is a simple technique and can be used on many types of outdoor projects. The only joint you have to learn is the half-lap. As you'll see, there are many ways to make this joint and you won't need a shop full of power tools to get perfect results.

The standard outdoor construction principles apply to this and all the other projects. Use waterproof exterior-rated adhesives and galvanized or stainless steel fasteners. Try to avoid joints or connections where pieces meet and form a natural trap for dirt and moisture. If you can't avoid a water trap, drill drainage holes, then soak the in side of those holes with an exterior rated finish.

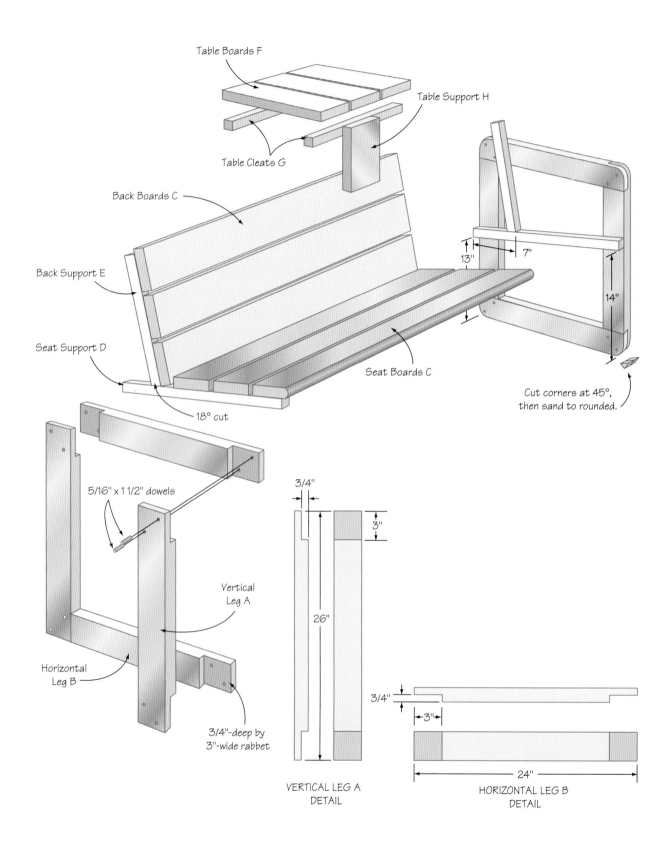

Table Boards F

Table Support H

Table Cleats G

Back Boards C

Back Support E

Seat Support D

Seat Boards C

18° cut

13"

7"

14"

Cut corners at 45°,
then sand to rounded.

5/16" x 1 1/2" dowels

Vertical
Leg A

Horizontal
Leg B

3/4"-deep by
3"-wide rabbet

3/4"

3"

26"

3/4"

3"

24"

VERTICAL LEG A
DETAIL

HORIZONTAL LEG B
DETAIL

CUTTING LIST • tête-à-tête bench

REF.	QTY.	PART	MATERIAL	THICK	WIDTH	LENGTH	COMMENTS
A	4	Vertical legs	Cedar	$1\frac{1}{2}$	3	26	
B	4	Horizontal legs	Cedar	$1\frac{1}{2}$	3	24	
C	6	Back and seat boards	Cedar	$1\frac{1}{2}$	$5\frac{1}{2}$	60	
D	2	Seat supports	Cedar	$1\frac{1}{2}$	$1\frac{1}{2}$	$23\frac{1}{2}$	
E	2	Back supports	Cedar	$1\frac{1}{2}$	$1\frac{1}{2}$	16	
F	3	Table boards	Cedar	$1\frac{1}{2}$	$5\frac{1}{2}$	18	
G	2	Table cleats	Cedar	$1\frac{1}{2}$	$1\frac{1}{2}$	15	
H	1	Table support	Cedar	$1\frac{1}{2}$	$5\frac{1}{2}$	$7\frac{1}{2}$	

Hardware and Supplies

$\frac{5}{16}$"-dia. dowel material

$2\frac{1}{2}$" Exterior-rated screws

Polyurethane glue

Sikkens Cetol 1 #078 Natural finish

REQUIRED **tools**

Table Saw or Circular Saw

Drill

Miter Box

Combination Square

Hammer

Screw Gun or Drivers

Sander or Sandpaper and Block

Router and Bits

Cutting a Half-Lap Joint

Half-lap joints, one of the more common woodworking joints, can be successfully completed using nothing more than a circular saw. All you need to do is simply make a series of repetitive cuts on the waste side of the board and remove the material using a chisel. The results are more than acceptable, and will work quite nicely when other woodworking power tools are not available.

If you have access to a table saw, however, follow along with these simple steps shown here to make your half-lap joints and you'll get professional results every time.

First, make a shoulder cut that's one-half the thickness of the board. The cut is placed 3" up from the end or at a distance equal to the width of the boards you will be joining.

Next, make your second cut to complete the cheek, using a tool like the Delta tenon jig or your own homemade version for the table saw — or the waste could be removed with a band saw.

You could even complete the joint in just one step by using a dado blade in a table saw. If it's a small half-lap joint, you can make the cuts on a regular table saw with a standard blade.

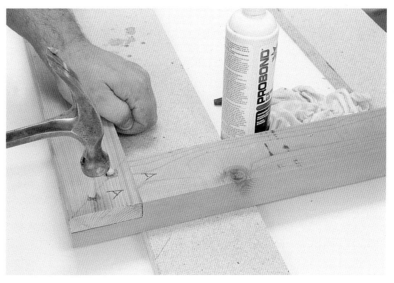

1 Cut the four vertical legs (A) and four horizontal legs (B) to size. Next, prepare the legs for assembly by forming a ¾"-deep by 3"-long rabbet on each end. The rabbet cuts are one-half of a half-lap joint. Dry fit the joints, forming two rectangles or leg loops. Then as shown here, drill two ⁵⁄₁₆"-diameter holes along a line 45° to the corner. Drill completely through both legs with a piece of scrap wood on the underside to prevent hole tear-out. Remember to mark each joint with witness marks so they can be assembled in the same order as they were drilled.

2 Use an exterior-rated adhesive and two ⁵⁄₁₆"-diameter dowels to secure each joint. Use dowels that will extend a little past each face so they can be sanded flush when the glue cures.

4 Soften the sharp edges of each cut with a sander. Then, use a ⅜" roundover bit in a router to ease the inside and outside edges on both faces of each assembly.

3 Miter each corner on both assemblies at 45°. Use a power or hand miter saw and make the cut ¾" from each outside corner.

5 Attach the seat supports (D) with 2½" screws and glue. The seat support is installed 13" from the bottom at the back of each loop and 14" at the front. This will create a slightly sloped seat for comfortable seating.

Tip

Always predrill screw holes before insertion. This practice is especially important in areas such as installing the seat and back supports because you are working near the end of a board. The supports will split without this pilot hole.

6 Attach the two back supports (E) next. They will need an 18° angle cut on one end. The angled or bottom end is secured with a 2½" screw and glued through the seat support with its front face 7" from the back end of the leg. Secure the top with two 2½" screws and exterior-rated adhesive.

Tip

You may want more or less of a back slope on your bench. If that's the case, alter the angle on the bottom of each support. You can find the right back slant for your project by measuring a favorite chair and experimenting a little before you glue the supports in place.

7 Cut and install the three back boards (C), spacing them ⅛" apart. Use glue and 2½" screws through the back support. Start with the first (lower) board resting on the seat support.

CONSTRUCTION NOTES

- The tête-à-tête bench is a straightforward project to build. Just about any wood is suitable.

- If you prefer a plain bench, omit the table section. Or if you want the bench a little wider, use longer seat and back boards.

- The amount of slant on the backrest as well as the slope on the seat is a matter of personal taste. If you prefer leaning back farther, change the back support angle. To be certain, try a few different seat and back support angle combinations until you find one that's right for you.

- Remember the golden rule with outdoor furniture projects: Never give dirt and moisture a place to collect. Wood rot is the enemy, so do everything you can to prevent it from happening. As I've said before, use weather-resistant hardware and waterproof glues and maintain the protective finish on all your projects. If you do, your projects will last for decades.

8 Install the seat boards (C) with glue and screws through the seat supports. Start the first board ⅛" away from the bottom back board to provide a space for water runoff.

9 Cut the three table boards (F) with one end of each angled at 18°. The table cleats (G) are secured to the underside with glue and screws. Space the table boards ⅛" apart and set the front cleat 2" back from the edge. The rear cleat is secured ½" back from the rear edge of the table boards. Before securing the table, round over the front outside corners with a belt sander to prevent injuries.

10 Attach the table support (H) to the assembly with 2½" screws and glue. Center the support on the front cleat. Then as shown here, install the table assembly with glue and screws by securing it from the underside and rear face of the back boards. At tach the table so it's slightly off level to allow proper drainage. Finally, sand the bench and apply a good-quality finish. I used Sikkens Cetol 1 #078 Natural to complete my project.

outdoor dining set

This is an easy-to-build dining set that's sturdy and won't cost you a small fortune for materials. But don't let the simplicity fool you, because the table and chairs will serve you well for many years.

I used construction-grade cedar for my set, but like all the other projects in this book, the choice of materials is optional. Most lumberyards allow you to select your own wood, so pick through the construction-grade pile and select the best pieces. You could build the set with select-grade lumber, but the costs will rise. The material choice here isn't as important as the quality of the hardware, adhesives and finish that you use.

If your budget limits you to a circular saw and a few hand tools, this is the project for you. Bring a few tools up to the cottage and build this outdoor dining set. But be careful not to show it off too much, because you may get a dozen orders from your neighbors.

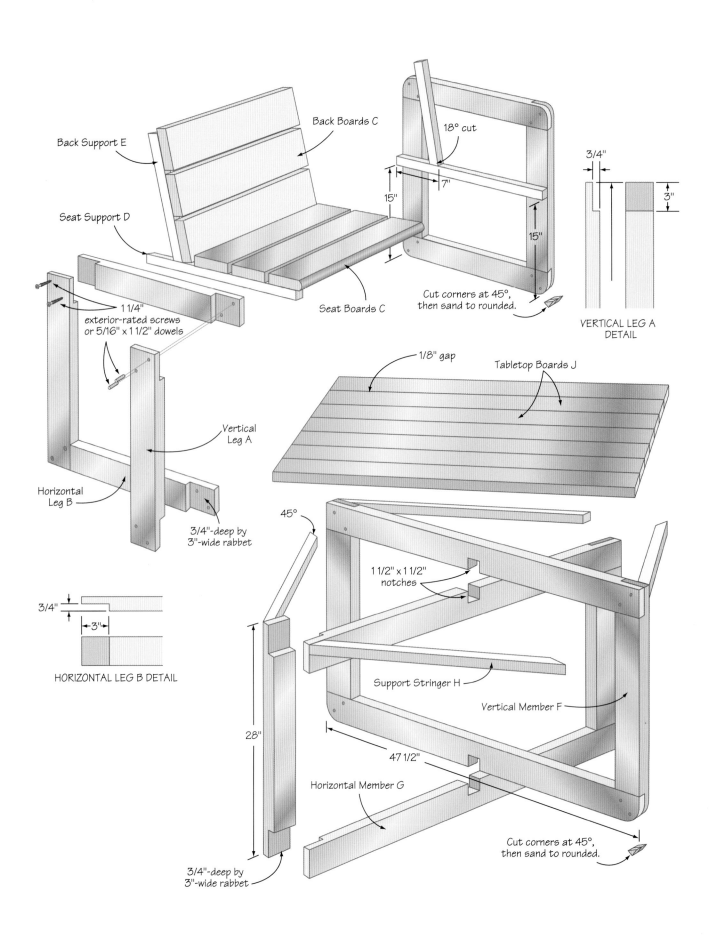

Back Support E

Back Boards C

18° cut

Seat Support D

15"

7"

15"

Cut corners at 45°, then sand to rounded.

Seat Boards C

3/4"

3"

VERTICAL LEG A DETAIL

1 1/4" exterior-rated screws or 5/16" x 1 1/2" dowels

1/8" gap

Tabletop Boards J

Vertical Leg A

Horizontal Leg B

3/4"-deep by 3"-wide rabbet

45°

1 1/2" x 1 1/2" notches

3/4"

3"

HORIZONTAL LEG B DETAIL

Support Stringer H

Vertical Member F

28"

47 1/2"

Horizontal Member G

3/4"-deep by 3"-wide rabbet

Cut corners at 45°, then sand to rounded.

CUTTING LIST • **outdoor dining set**

REF.	QTY.	PART	MATERIAL	THICK	WIDTH	LENGTH	COMMENTS
Chair (materials listed for one chair only)							
A	4	Vertical legs	Cedar	$1\frac{1}{2}$	3	26	
B	4	Horizontal legs	Cedar	$1\frac{1}{2}$	3	24	
C	6	Back and seat boards	Cedar	$1\frac{1}{2}$	$5\frac{1}{2}$	23	
D	2	Seat supports	Cedar	$1\frac{1}{2}$	$1\frac{1}{2}$	24	
E	2	Back supports	Cedar	$1\frac{1}{2}$	$1\frac{1}{2}$	16	
Table							
F	4	Vertical members	Cedar	$1\frac{1}{2}$	3	$47\frac{1}{2}$	
G	4	Horizontal members	Cedar	$1\frac{1}{2}$	3	28	
H	4	Support stringers	Cedar	$1\frac{1}{2}$	$1\frac{1}{2}$	$32\frac{1}{2}$	45° cuts at both ends
J	7	Tabletop boards	Cedar	$1\frac{1}{2}$	$5\frac{1}{2}$	40	

Hardware and Supplies

$1\frac{1}{4}$" Exterior-rated screws

$2\frac{1}{2}$" Exterior-rated screws

Polyurethane glue

Sikkens Cetol 1 #077 Cedar finish

REQUIRED **tools**

Table Saw or Circular Saw

Drill

Miter Box

Combination Square

Hammer

Screw Gun or Drivers

Sander or Sandpaper and Block

Router and Bits

BUILDING THE CHAIR

Saving Time With a Tenoning Jig

1 Cut the four vertical legs (A) and horizontal legs (B) to length. Each leg requires a ¾"-deep by 3"-long rabbet on both ends. You can make the cuts with hand tools or with a table saw, router table, radial arm saw or circular saw. If you decide to use a circular saw, set the blade depth to ¾". Make a series of cuts across the face in the joint field and, as shown here, use a hammer to break away the waste. Then clean the joints with a sharp chisel.

If you plan to make a number of sets for friends and family, a tenoning jig, as shown above, is a great accessory for your table saw. It easily and accurately cuts rabbets and tenons. It's one of my favorite tools because of the accuracy and safety features. And best of all, it isn't that expensive!

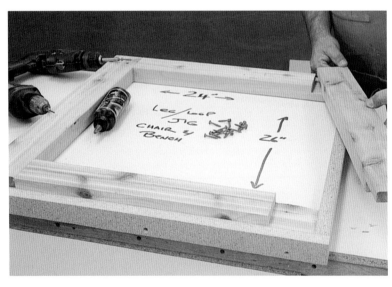

3 Sand the frames and cut each corner at 45°. The miters should be 1" back from the corner intersection of each leg. Use a handsaw or power miter to cut the corners.

2 Join two vertical and two horizontal legs to make one side assembly. Use waterproof adhesive and two 1¼" exterior-rated screws at each joint. You can also use wood dowels for the joinery following the process discussed for the tête-à-tête bench. Each leg loop assembly should be 26" high and 24" wide. Install the screws 1" apart and 1½" in from the outside corner of each joint.

Tip

If you plan to build a few chairs, the tête-à-tête bench or just a straight bench, remember that the leg loop assemblies are all the same. Construct an assembly frame jig with a scrap piece of any sheet goods and attach four boards to form an outside perimeter of 24" x 26". This jig will ensure that all your leg loop assemblies are accurately constructed.

4 Use a ⅜" roundover bit in a router to soften the inner and outer faces on both assemblies. Sand the sharp mitered corners with a belt sander to soften the cuts. Then as shown here, install the two seat supports (D) with their top surface 15" above the bottom of each assembly. Use glue and two 2½" screws per joint.

Tip

Be sure to predrill holes in the seat and back supports. You will be installing screws very close to the ends of these boards, and they will split without a pilot hole.

5 The bottom of the two back supports (E) must be cut at 18°. This cut will create the back slant needed for comfortable seating. Attach the boards with the longest dimension of the angle 7" from the rear of the seat supports. Use glue and 2½" screws to secure the back supports. Driving the screw through the seat support makes the lower connection. Be careful at this point because you are now creating a right and left assembly.

6 Each chair requires six boards (C) to form the seat and back. Start by installing the bottom back board, resting it on the seat supports. Attach all the boards with glue and 2½" screws from the rear and underside. The boards are flush with the outside face of the supports. Space them all ⅛" apart. Let the adhesive set up, and perform the final sanding on your chairs.

BUILDING THE TABLE

1 Prepare the vertical members (F) and the horizontal members (G) by cutting a ¾"-deep by 3"-long rabbet on both ends of all the boards. Then cut a 1½"-deep by 1½"-wide dado centered on each of the horizontal members. Assemble the frames as shown here by joining two vertical to two horizontal members. One frame must have the dadoes open toward the inside, and the other frame has the dadoes facing out. Use glue and 1¼" screws to assemble the frames. However, one horizontal member on one of the frames should be attached with screws only. This will allow removal when the frames are joined.

2 Sand the frames, and miter only the bottom corners at 45°. Round over the inner and outer face of each frame with a ⅜" roundover router bit. Remove the horizontal member that was only screwed from one of the frames. Then as shown here, join them by fitting the dadoes inside each other. Re-install the top member using glue and screws, making sure the dadoes fit properly. Use glue and 2½" screws to lock the frames together at the dado joints.

3 Align the support stringers (H) flush with the tops of the frames. Secure them to the frame with glue and 2½" screws.

Tip

The easiest way to attach the table-top boards is by laying them on a flat surface with ⅛" spacers between each board. Center the frame on the boards so the stringers run parallel with each side and install the screws.

CONSTRUCTION NOTES

- Changing the length of all horizontal frame members easily alters the table size. Or you can create a round table if you prefer that look.
- The table can be fitted with an umbrella by drilling a hole next to the intersection of the two horizontal frame members. If you drill the hole accurately, the frame can be used to anchor the umbrella to the table.
- Quite a few design options are available. Chair seats can be slanted, the backrest angle can be easily changed, and the chair width is variable.
- You can build an oval table by altering the frame dimensions. One long and the other short, with the appropriate stringers, will allow you to build a large table to seat six or eight. However, you will need extra chairs.
- And finally, you can further reduce the construction costs by using pressure-treated lumber. This material is particularly suitable if you plan to paint the set with a solid-colored exterior finish.

4 Center the frame on the seven tabletop boards (J), spacing them at ⅛". Use glue and 2½" screws from the underside to secure the boards. Sand the table and soften the sharp edges to prevent cuts and scrapes should anyone bump the corners. Apply a good exterior finish, making sure all the surfaces are coated. I used Sikkens Cetol 1 #077 Cedar to finish my set.

classic picnic table

This classic project seats six comfortably and is built to take a great deal of abuse. It isn't a complicated project to build and doesn't require a large outlay of money, but it's one of the handiest pieces of outdoor furniture you'll ever own.

If you're like me, you've probably bumped into the corners on a standard table and received a nice little scar. To prevent that, I've softened the table corners and seat ends with a radius. I guarantee this table won't bite back.

I used standard construction-grade cedar for my table and made sure all the hardware was exterior rated. The adhesive is one of the new waterproof one-part polyurethanes. So, with regular maintenance, this table should be around for many years.

Nothing is more annoying than sitting on a hot screw head. For that reason, always try to cover the hardware with wood plugs or install them from the underside. This project is no different — all the screws are installed from the bottom.

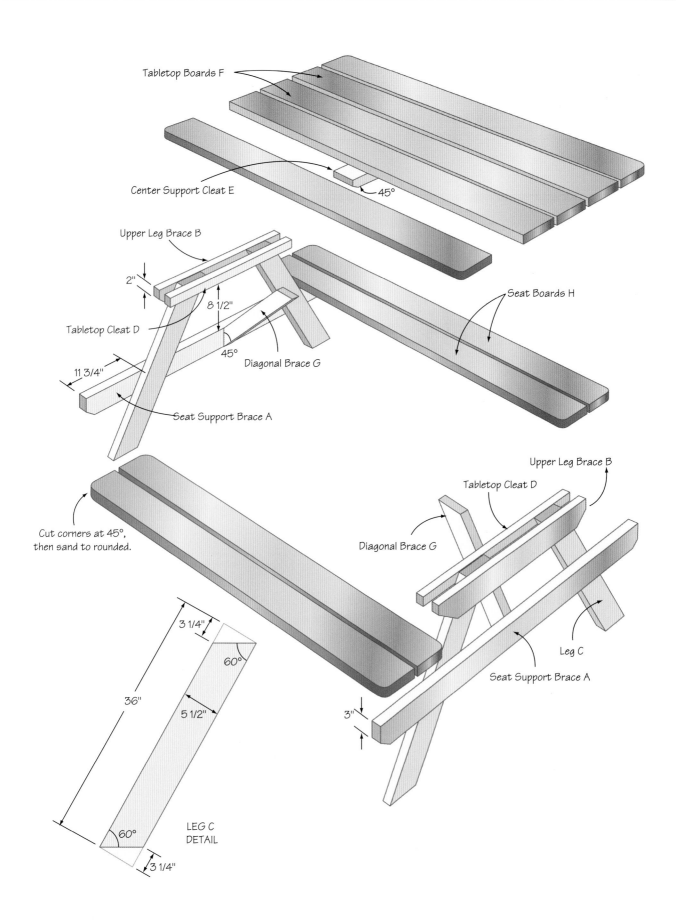

Tabletop Boards F

Center Support Cleat E

45°

Upper Leg Brace B

2"

8 1/2"

Tabletop Cleat D

45°

11 3/4"

Diagonal Brace G

Seat Support Brace A

Seat Boards H

Cut corners at 45°,
then sand to rounded.

Upper Leg Brace B

Tabletop Cleat D

Diagonal Brace G

Leg C

Seat Support Brace A

3"

3 1/4"

60°

36"

5 1/2"

60°

LEG C
DETAIL

3 1/4"

CUTTING LIST • **classic picnic table**

REF.	QTY.	PART	MATERIAL	THICK	WIDTH	LENGTH	COMMENTS
A	2	Seat support braces	Cedar	$1\frac{1}{2}$	$5\frac{1}{2}$	$58\frac{1}{2}$	
B	2	Upper leg braces	Cedar	$1\frac{1}{2}$	$3\frac{1}{2}$	$28\frac{1}{4}$	
C	4	Legs	Cedar	$1\frac{1}{2}$	$5\frac{1}{2}$	36	
D	2	Tabletop cleats	Cedar	$1\frac{1}{2}$	$1\frac{1}{2}$	$28\frac{1}{4}$	
E	1	Center support cleat	Cedar	$1\frac{1}{2}$	$3\frac{1}{2}$	28	
F	5	Tabletop boards	Cedar	$1\frac{1}{2}$	$5\frac{1}{2}$	72	
G	2	Diagonal braces	Cedar	$1\frac{1}{2}$	$3\frac{1}{2}$	24	
H	4	Seat boards	Cedar	$1\frac{1}{2}$	$5\frac{1}{2}$	72	

Hardware and Supplies

$2\frac{1}{2}$" Exterior-rated screws

Polyurethane glue

Sikkens Cetol 1 #077 Cedar finish

REQUIRED **tools**

Table Saw or Circular Saw

Drill

Jigsaw

Combination Square

Hammer

Screw Gun or Drivers

Sander or Sandpaper and Block

1 First, spend some time prepping your pieces. Cut the seat support braces (A) to length. The lower miters on each end are 45° cuts and begin 3" down from the top edge. Cut the two upper leg braces (B) to length; these also require 45° miters beginning 2" down from their top edges. Also cut all four legs (C) to length; these require 60° miters on each end. Then begin the leg assembly steps by attaching two legs to the upper leg braces with glue and 2½" screws. Align the legs so they intersect the miters on the braces. Make sure the top edges of the legs are flush with the top edge of the braces. Next, as shown here, attach the seat support braces (A) to the legs, leaving 11¾" overhang on both ends. The top edge of the seat support should be 8½" below the bottom edge of the upper leg brace.

2 The tabletop boards (F) will be secured through cleats (D) that are attached to the inside of the legs. Use glue and screws to secure these two cleats flush with the top of each leg pair.

Tip

Cut a piece of scrap sheet that's 8½" wide. Use it as a jig to align and properly space the seat support brace to the upper leg brace.

3 Lay the tabletop boards (F) on a flat surface and separate them with ¼"-wide spacers. Remember to put the best faces down. Attach the leg assemblies to the tabletop boards with glue and 2½" screws driven through the cleats. The leg assemblies are located 4" in from each end.

4 Cut and attach a center support cleat (E) to the underside of the tabletop boards in the center of those boards. Install one screw in each table board. This cleat will help to keep the top surface of the table flat. Ease the lower face corners on both ends of the cleat with a sander to remove the sharp edges. Then as shown here, attach the two diagonal braces (G) to support the leg assemblies. Both ends of the braces are mitered at 45°. The braces are properly located when the leg assemblies are at 90° to the tabletop boards.

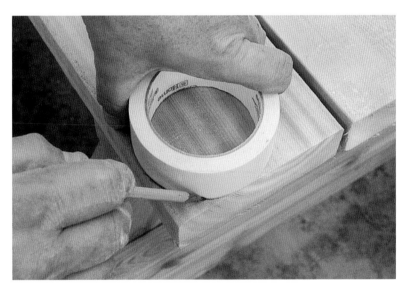

6 Locate something in your shop that's about 4" in diameter. Use it to draw an arc on the four tabletop corners, as well as the eight seat corners. Cut the arcs with a jigsaw and sand them smooth. Continue with the final sanding and apply a good-quality exterior finish. I used Sikkens Cetol 1 #077 Cedar.

5 Install the seat boards (H) on the seat support braces (A). Place them so they are aligned with the tabletop boards. And space them ¼" apart to allow for water drainage. The outside board should be ¼" past the seat support end. Use glue and 2½" screws driven at an angle, through the seat support inside face, into the seat board bottom.

CONSTRUCTION NOTES

- If you plan to paint the table a solid color, use the less-expensive pressure-treated woods. Many of the tables offered for sale at the home centers use construction-grade spruce, fir or pine. If you plan to use these species of wood, be very sure all the surfaces receive a good coating of protective finish. Cedar is often the wood of choice because it has some rot-resistant properties not found in other softwoods.

- Don't skimp on the adhesives or fasteners — use only weather-resistant products. Rot often begins with rusted screws and nails, so you won't be saving any money in the long run.

- These tables have a history of racking or becoming "wobbly" so use screws in place of nails. And don't be shy about using too many fasteners. As my carpenter father often said, "Better one nail too many than one too few."

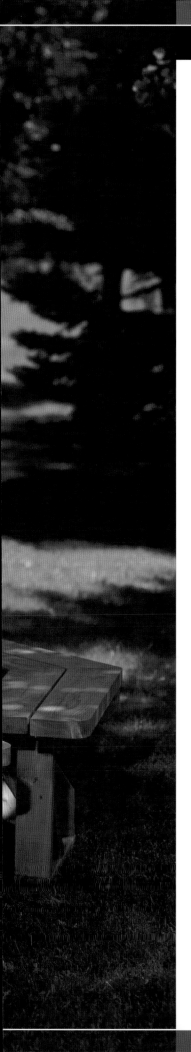

octagonal picnic table

If you have a large family or a lot of friends dropping over for lunch, then this table is the project for you. It will seat eight in style, and though it looks complicated, it's quite easy to build — just take each process one at a time and you'll breeze right through.

This project can be an exercise in mathematics. Just remember the basic rule of circles. You can calculate any angle required for the number of divisions in a circle by dividing it into 360. An octagon has 8 sides, so 360 divided by 8 equals 45. Each angle at its intersection is therefore 45°, so two 22.5° angles are needed to create a 45° intersection.

One word of caution to keep in mind with this project is its size. Because it's almost eight feet across the diagonal, it could present a problem removing it from your shop. Plan ahead — unless you want an octagonal picnic table in your shop on a permanent basis.

I used cedar for my table because it's a good outdoor wood, but almost any species will work as long as it's well protected against the elements.

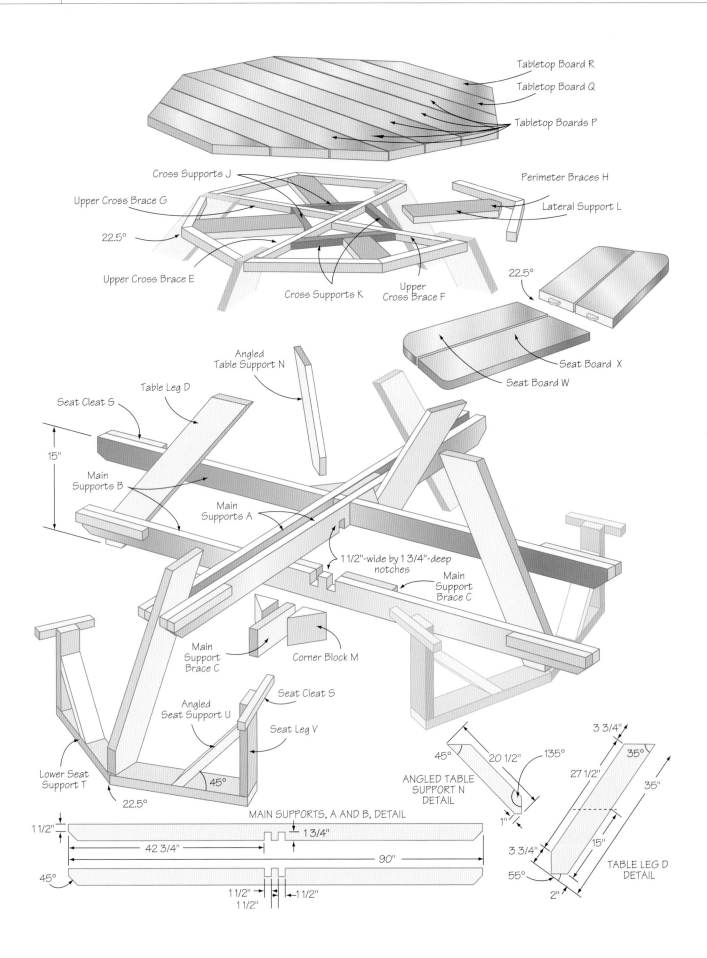

Tabletop Board R
Tabletop Board Q
Tabletop Boards P

Cross Supports J
Upper Cross Brace G
Perimeter Braces H
Lateral Support L
22.5°
Upper Cross Brace E
Cross Supports K
Upper Cross Brace F
22.5°
Seat Board X
Seat Board W

Angled Table Support N
Seat Cleat S
Table Leg D
15"
Main Supports B
Main Supports A
1 1/2"-wide by 1 3/4"-deep notches
Main Support Brace C
Main Support Brace C
Corner Block M
Seat Cleat S
Angled Seat Support U
Seat Leg V
Lower Seat Support T
45°
22.5°

MAIN SUPPORTS, A AND B, DETAIL
1 1/2"
1 3/4"
42 3/4"
90"
45°
1 1/2"
1 1/2"
1 1/2"

45°
20 1/2"
135°
ANGLED TABLE SUPPORT N DETAIL
1"

3 3/4"
35°
27 1/2"
35"
3 3/4"
15"
55°
2"
TABLE LEG D DETAIL

CUTTING LIST • **octagonal picnic table**

REF.	QTY.	PART	MATERIAL	THICK	WIDTH	LENGTH	COMMENTS
A	2	Main supports	Cedar	$1\frac{1}{2}$	$3\frac{1}{2}$	90	
B	2	Main supports	Cedar	$1\frac{1}{2}$	$3\frac{1}{2}$	90	
C	4	Main support braces	Cedar	$1\frac{1}{2}$	$3\frac{1}{2}$	6	
D	4	Table legs	Cedar	$1\frac{1}{2}$	$5\frac{1}{2}$	35	
E	1	Upper cross brace	Cedar	$1\frac{1}{2}$	$1\frac{1}{2}$	46	
F	1	Upper cross brace	Cedar	$1\frac{1}{2}$	$1\frac{1}{2}$	$20\frac{3}{4}$	
G	1	Upper cross brace	Cedar	$1\frac{1}{2}$	$1\frac{1}{2}$	$23\frac{1}{2}$	
H	8	Perimeter braces	Cedar	$1\frac{1}{2}$	$1\frac{1}{2}$	$18\frac{1}{4}$	
J	2	Cross supports	Cedar	$1\frac{1}{2}$	$1\frac{1}{2}$	$14\frac{5}{8}$	
K	2	Cross supports	Cedar	$1\frac{1}{2}$	$1\frac{1}{2}$	18	
L	4	Lateral supports	Cedar	$1\frac{1}{2}$	$3\frac{1}{2}$	18	
M	4	Corner blocks	Cedar	$1\frac{1}{2}$	$1\frac{1}{2}$	$3\frac{1}{2}$	
N	4	Angled table supports	Cedar	$1\frac{1}{2}$	$3\frac{1}{2}$	$21\frac{1}{2}$	
P	5	Tabletop boards	Cedar	$1\frac{1}{2}$	$5\frac{1}{2}$	53	
Q	2	Tabletop boards	Cedar	$1\frac{1}{2}$	$5\frac{1}{2}$	49	
R	2	Tabletop boards	Cedar	$1\frac{1}{2}$	$5\frac{1}{2}$	37	
S	16	Seat cleats	Cedar	$1\frac{1}{2}$	$1\frac{1}{2}$	$9\frac{1}{2}$	
T	8	Lower seat supports	Cedar	$1\frac{1}{2}$	$1\frac{1}{2}$	18	
U	8	Angled seat supports	Cedar	$1\frac{1}{2}$	$3\frac{1}{2}$	12	
V	8	Seat legs	Cedar	$1\frac{1}{2}$	$3\frac{1}{2}$	15	
W	8	Seat boards	Cedar	$1\frac{1}{2}$	$5\frac{1}{2}$	$25\frac{3}{16}$	
X	8	Seat boards	Cedar	$1\frac{1}{2}$	$5\frac{1}{2}$	$27\frac{1}{2}$	

Hardware and Supplies

$2\frac{1}{2}$" Exterior-rated screws

Polyurethane glue

Sikkens Cetol 1 #078 Natural finish

2" Exterior-rated (galvanized) nails

REQUIRED **tools**

Table Saw or Circular Saw

Drill

Jigsaw

Miter Box

Combination Square

Hammer

Screw Gun or Drivers

Sander or Sandpaper and Block

1 Cut the four main supports (A and B). Trim them to size and cut the miters on each end prior to cutting the notches. The four supports will be joined with half-lap joints. The main supports (A) require notches on the bottom as indicated in the drawing, and the supports (B) need the notches on the top edge. The notch cuts are spaced to leave a 1½" square in the middle, which will permit an umbrella to be installed if needed. So as shown here, cut the notches with a jigsaw. Holes wide enough for the jigsaw blade, drilled at the inside bottom corners of each notch, will allow you to turn the saw and complete the cuts.

2 Join the four main supports as shown using exterior adhesive. Drive a 2½" screw through the top of each joint.

3 Install the four main support braces (C) at the inside corners of the supports. Secure them with glue and screws to strengthen the center joints.

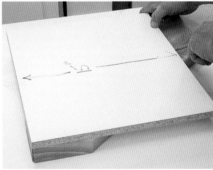

4 Prepare the four table legs (D) as detailed. Mark a guide line on both sides of each leg 15" from the leg bottoms. This line must be parallel with the top cut.

Tip

Make laying out the leg guide line easier by using a board cut 15" square. Align it with the bottom cut and flush with both edges, then draw the line.

5 Secure the legs between each set of main supports. The back of each leg is 12" from the end of the main supports. Be sure that the top edges of the supports are aligned with the 15" guide mark on each leg. Secure the legs with glue and four 2½" screws per side.

6 Cut and install the upper cross brace (E). Leave 1½" between the ends of the brace and backs of the legs on each end.

7 Attach the remaining upper cross braces (F and G). Secure them to opposite leg faces so the centers will be staggered. Use glue and screws to fasten the braces.

8 The eight perimeter braces (H) must have their ends mitered at 22.5°. Attach them to the legs with glue and screws. Angle-trim the cross braces where they interfere with the perimeter braces. The end of each perimeter brace is aligned flush with the outside face of the leg.

9 Install the four cross supports (J and K) as shown. They are needed to provide support for the cross braces and extra attachment surface for the tabletop boards. Their position is not critical.

10 The four lateral supports (L) stiffen the perimeter braces. Rough-cut the four pieces to 18". Mark them in place to determine the exact position of the two 22.5° cuts where they meet the perimeter brace. Use glue and screws to secure the supports.

11 The four corner blocks (M) are glued and nailed in place.

12 Cut the angled table supports (N) as shown in the drawing. Attach them to the corner blocks and the underside of the lateral supports. Miter these supports at 45° on both ends. And cut one end at 90° to the miter so it will be flush with the bottom edge of the corner block. Use glue and screws, making sure the perimeter braces are level.

13 Lay the nine tabletop boards (P, Q and R) on a flat surface with the larger boards in the center. Apply glue to the table frame and center it on the boards. Align opposing ends of the perimeter braces so they are parallel and equally spaced on the 37"-long outside boards. Space the tabletop boards ⅛" apart and secure the frame to the boards with 2½" screws.

14 Outline an octagon on top of the tabletop boards 2" larger than the perimeter braces on all faces. Once you are satisfied that the tabletop outline is correct, cut the octagon with a circular saw.

15 Attach eight of the seat cleats (S) with adhesive to the main supports. Install them flush with the ends and tops of the main supports.

16 The eight lower seat supports (T) are joined in pairs at their 22.5°-mitered ends. They can be joined with adhesive and biscuits, dowels or pocket screw holes.

17 Assemble the four seat support assemblies (from pieces T, U and V) as shown. Use glue and screws for each joint. Attach the remaining seat cleats centered on the top outside face of each seat leg (V).

18 Secure the seat assemblies to each table leg (D). The table leg sits on top of the assembly and must be aligned 22.5° to the leg face. To simplify the alignment, cut a scrap piece of 2×4 at 22.5°. Use it to accurately align each seat assembly to the leg side. Secure the joint with glue and four 2½" screws through the leg face and into the lower seat support boards (T).

19 Cut the 16 seat boards (W and X) as detailed in the cutting list. Each requires a 22.5° miter on one end. Dry fit the seat boards with the shorter ones on the inside. All the boards are aligned 22.5° to the table leg sides. Mark a line on each main support and through the seat cleats using the correctly positioned outer seat boards as a guide. Cut the main support and cleats with a circular saw. This angle cut will match the outside edge of the seat boards.

CONSTRUCTION NOTES

- Take your time building this table and use good-quality glue and fasteners. It's big, heavy, and will be supporting the weight of eight people, so make all your joints accurately.
- You will most likely move it by lifting on the seat assemblies, so a few extra screws at those joints will be helpful.
- If you're concerned about the seat-assembly-to-leg connections, add small corner blocks to strengthen those joints. But the force is downward on the seats, so that joint should be fine unless you plan to move the table often.

20 Use any easily available, round object about 4" in diameter. Draw an arc on all 16 seat corners and cut along the line with a jigsaw. Sand the arc smooth with a belt sander. This removes potentially dangerous sharp corners. Complete the table construction by giving it a final sanding. Apply a good-quality finish to protect the wood. I used Sikkens Cetol 1 #078 Natural to finish my table.

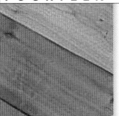

chaise lounge

While on a recent vacation, we enjoyed the beach with many other vacationers who were reading and relaxing on chaise lounges. The lounges were comfortable, had an adjustable backrest, and were perfect for reading or a nap. But I had a problem finding a resting place for my drink and book. So I decided to build one of my own, complete with a pullout table.

This project is the result. It's built with construction-grade western red cedar. It's an ideal outdoor wood, but others, like redwood and cypress, would also be suitable. And the pullout tray is a feature you won't find on many models. The gently curved sides and adjustable headrest make this project well worth quality-control testing for an extended period of time.

This is another one of those projects that's reasonably priced. Check the cost on retail versions and you'll soon be convinced that this home-built chaise is well worth making.

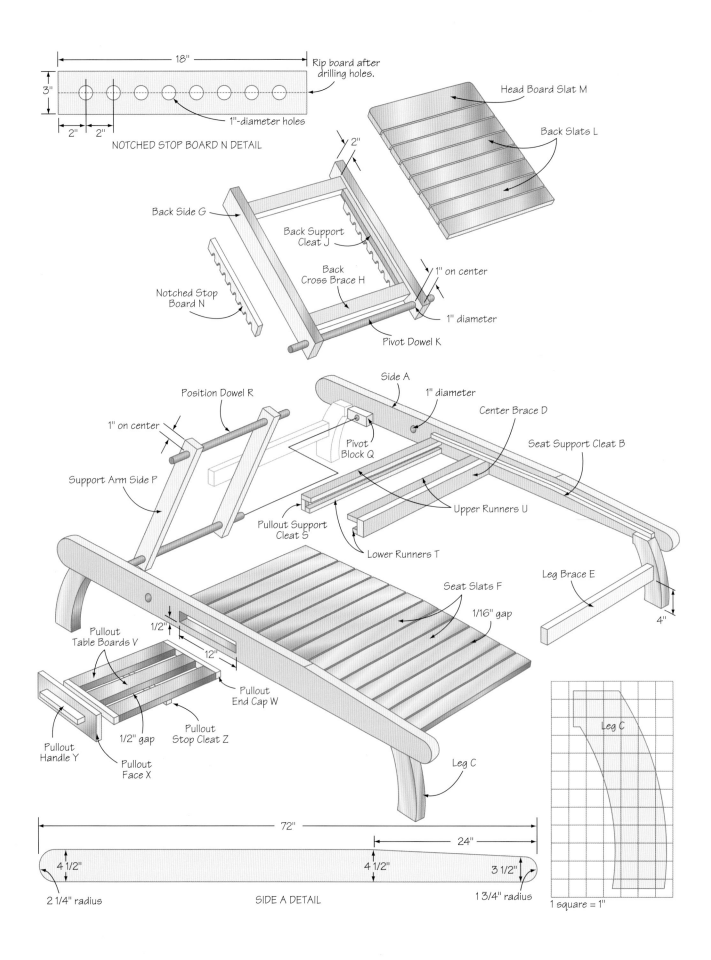

18"

3"

Rip board after drilling holes.

2" 2"

1"-diameter holes

NOTCHED STOP BOARD N DETAIL

Head Board Slat M

Back Slats L

2"

Back Side G

Back Support Cleat J

1" on center

Back Cross Brace H

Notched Stop Board N

1" diameter

Pivot Dowel K

Side A

1" diameter

Center Brace D

Position Dowel R

Seat Support Cleat B

1" on center

Pivot Block Q

Support Arm Side P

Pullout Support Cleat S

Upper Runners U

Lower Runners T

Seat Slats F

1/16" gap

Leg Brace E

4"

1/2"

Pullout Table Boards V

12"

Pullout End Cap W

Pullout Stop Cleat Z

1/2" gap

Pullout Handle Y

Pullout Face X

Leg C

72"

24"

4 1/2"

4 1/2"

3 1/2"

2 1/4" radius

SIDE A DETAIL

1 3/4" radius

Leg C

1 square = 1"

CUTTING LIST • **chaise lounge**

REF.	QTY.	PART	MATERIAL	THICK	WIDTH	LENGTH	COMMENTS
A	2	Sides	Cedar	$1\frac{1}{2}$	$4\frac{1}{2}$	72	
B	2	Seat support cleats	Cedar	$\frac{3}{4}$	$\frac{3}{4}$	48	
C	4	Leg blanks	Cedar	$1\frac{1}{2}$	$5\frac{1}{2}$	11	
D	1	Center brace	Cedar	$1\frac{1}{2}$	$2\frac{1}{2}$	23	
E	2	Leg braces	Cedar	$1\frac{1}{2}$	$2\frac{1}{2}$	20	
F	14	Seat slats	Cedar	$\frac{3}{4}$	$3\frac{1}{2}$	23	
G	2	Back sides	Cedar	$1\frac{1}{2}$	3	30	
H	2	Back cross braces	Cedar	$1\frac{1}{2}$	$2\frac{1}{4}$	$19\frac{3}{4}$	
J	2	Back support cleats	Cedar	$\frac{3}{4}$	$\frac{3}{4}$	$22\frac{3}{4}$	
K	1	Pivot dowel	Cedar	1 dia.		26	
L	7	Back slats	Cedar	$\frac{3}{4}$	$3\frac{1}{2}$	$19\frac{3}{4}$	
M	1	Headboard slat	Cedar	$\frac{3}{4}$	$5\frac{1}{2}$	$19\frac{3}{4}$	
N	1	Notched stop board	Cedar	$\frac{3}{4}$	3	18	
P	2	Support arm sides	Cedar	$1\frac{1}{2}$	$1\frac{1}{2}$	12	
Q	2	Pivot blocks	Cedar	$1\frac{1}{2}$	$1\frac{1}{2}$	4	
R	2	Position dowels	Cedar	1 dia.		$19\frac{1}{2}$	
S	2	Pullout support cleats	Cedar	$\frac{3}{4}$	$\frac{3}{4}$	$2\frac{1}{2}$	
T	2	Lower runners	Cedar	$\frac{3}{4}$	$\frac{3}{4}$	23	
U	2	Upper runners	Cedar	$\frac{3}{4}$	$1\frac{1}{2}$	$21\frac{1}{2}$	
V	3	Pullout table boards	Cedar	$\frac{3}{4}$	$3\frac{1}{2}$	22	
W	2	Pullout end caps	Cedar	$\frac{3}{4}$	$\frac{3}{4}$	$11\frac{1}{2}$	
X	1	Pullout face	Cedar	$\frac{3}{4}$	$2\frac{1}{2}$	14	
Y	1	Pullout handle	Cedar	$\frac{3}{4}$	1	$9\frac{1}{2}$	
Z	1	Pullout stop cleat	Cedar	$\frac{3}{4}$	1	$9\frac{1}{2}$	

Hardware and Supplies

$2\frac{1}{2}$" Exterior-rated screws

2" Exterior-rated screws

$1\frac{1}{4}$" Exterior-rated screws

1" Exterior-rated screws

Brad nails

Wood plugs

Polyurethane glue

Sikkens Cetol 1 #078 Natural finish

REQUIRED **tools**

Table Saw or Circular Saw

Drill

Miter Box

Combination Square

Jigsaw

Hammer

Screw Gun or Drivers

Sander or Sandpaper and Block

Router Bits

1 Prepare the two sides (A). Cut the radius ends and taper with a jigsaw or band saw. Then round over the edges and ends with a ⅜" roundover bit in a router.

Tip

Cut both sides from 1x6 lumber. Save the waste strips, as they can be used in step 2 as seat support cleats.

2 Mark a line on the inside face of both side boards. This line is ¾" below the top edge of both boards and begins 2" from the foot end. Use a combination square and follow the curve with your line. Then as shown here, attach the two seat support cleats (B) to the sides. The cleats are thin enough to bend and follow the previously marked guide line. Begin the slats 2" from the foot end and attach with glue and 2" exterior-rated screws. These thin cleats can easily split, so drill pilot holes for the screws. Install the screws every 8" along the cleats.

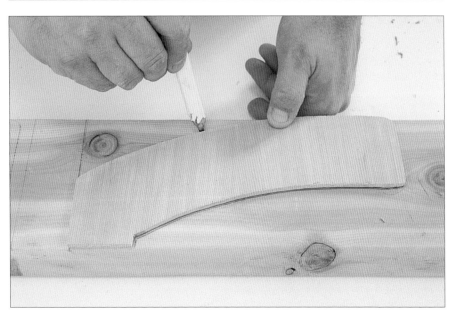

3 Cut the four legs (C) from the leg blanks as detailed in the cutting list. Create a pattern so that all legs will be identical. Follow the diagram to form the pattern. It isn't critical that your legs match the drawing exactly, but try to draw them as close as possible. Cut the legs using a band saw or jigsaw. Before installing the legs, round over the two curves, as well as the bottom edges.

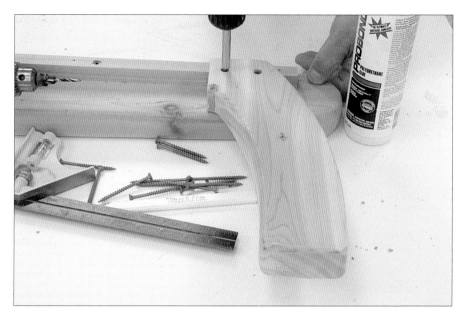

4 Attach the legs to the side boards using glue and 2½" screws. The outside upper corner of each leg is installed 6" from the side ends. The top flat surface of each leg is 1½" down from the top edge of the side boards.

5 Install the center brace (D) at the 36" mark on each side. The brace should be attached tightly under the seat support cleats (B). Use glue and two 2½" screws per joint, through the outside of the side board, and fill the counterbored holes with wood plugs.

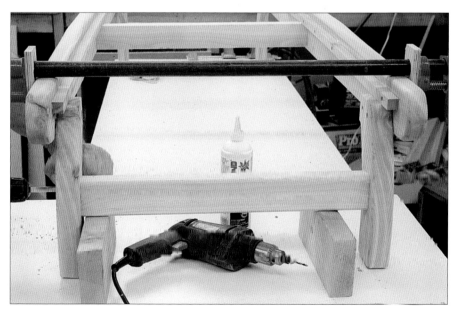

6 The two leg braces (E) span the distance between each leg set. Cut them to length and round over all the edges with a ⅜" router bit. They are attached 4" up from the bottom of each leg, using glue and two 2½" screws per joint. Drill counterbored holes on the outside of each leg into the ends of the braces. Fill the holes with wood plugs. The leg braces should be centered on each inside leg face.

Tip

Cut 4" spacer blocks to help align the legs. It's easier to locate the braces accurately with blocks rather than trying to hold them in place.

7 Prepare the 14 seat slats (F) by cutting to length and rounding over each upper end on all the boards with a ⅜" roundover bit in a router. The first slat at the foot end also requires its outside edge rounded over. Install it so the outside edge is ½" past the seat support cleats. I butted my boards together because the wood I'm using has a high moisture content. It wasn't kiln dried, so I expect some shrinkage. If your wood is dry, space the boards 1⁄16" apart. Trim the last board so it stops flush with the end of the seat support cleats. Glue and screw the boards in place with 1" screws. Drill the pilot and counterbored holes so they can be filled with wood plugs.

8 Cut the two back sides (G). Sand and round over all the edges on both pieces. The two back cross braces (H) join the back sides. They are secured with glue and 2½" screws. As shown here, drill and counter-bore screw holes through the outside face of each back side and drive the screws into each brace. Locate them 2" in from each end and flush with the bottom edge of the side boards.

9 The two back support cleats (J) run between the back cross braces (H). Attach them with glue and 2" screws, flush with the upper edge of the braces.

10 Drill a 1"-diameter hole through one end of each back side board (G). The hole is centered 1" from the end and in the middle of each face. Clamp the back assembly in place with ⅛" spacers on each side. Position it ½" away from the fixed seat slat so it can move freely. Then as shown here, use the previously drilled holes in the back assembly as a guide to locate and drill holes in the side boards (A). Remove the back assembly and drill a 1"-diameter hole through each side board.

11 Cut the 26"-long pivot dowel (K). Push it through the two sides and back assembly so it's flush with the two outside faces. Apply glue to the ends that are in the two side board holes only. Prepare the headboard slat (M) by cutting a small arc at each outside corner to remove the sharp edges. Round over the ends of all the back slats (L), as well as the outside edges of the bottom and head boards. Then as shown here, use glue and 1¼" screws in counterbored holes to install the back slats. Install the bottom back slat first, aligned flush with the ends of the back side boards. Fill the counterbored holes with wood plugs.

12 Begin building the adjustable back mechanism by cutting a notched stop board (N). Drill a series of eight 1"-diameter holes along its center line. The holes begin 2" from each end and are centered 2" apart. Cut board N down the center after drilling the holes. The result will be two boards with "half" holes. Then as shown here, attach the boards using glue and 2" screws to the inside face of each back side. Position these notched boards so they both touch the bottom cross brace.

Tip

Use a small drill bit to locate the center of each hole in the side boards. Drill the 1" hole from both sides, meeting in the middle, to prevent tear out and splintering at the hole edge.

13 The adjustable support arm is constructed with two sides (P), two position dowels (R), and two pivot blocks (Q). The pivot blocks require a 1"-diameter hole centered on the block. And the support arm sides require a 1"-diameter hole centered 1" from each end. The pivot blocks should rotate freely on each dowel, and the arms are "pinned" to the dowels with 1¼" screws. Then as shown here, install the support arm assembly by attaching the pivot blocks to the inside face of each side board. Position the blocks flush with the bottom edge of the sides and back against the legs. Use 2½" screws in pilot holes to secure the blocks.

14 Cut a 1"-wide slot, 12" long, in one side rail. The pullout can be installed on either side, so locate the slotted opening accordingly. The lower edge of the slot should be 1½" above the bottom edge of the side rail. Cut the slot between the center brace and headboard end of the lounge. The slot begins tight to the center brace. Use a 1"-diameter bit to drill holes at both ends of the slot and complete the cut with a jigsaw.

15 The pullout support is made with two upper runners (U), which are glued and nailed to the underside of the slats. The lower runners (T) are installed 1" below the upper runners. One runner is attached to the center brace, and the other is attached 1" below the upper runner using the pullout support cleats (S). The runners are spaced 12" apart in line with the side slot cutout. Use glue and brad nails to install the runners and cleats.

16 Build the pullout assembly as detailed. Attach the end caps (W) to the table boards (V) with glue and nails. Prepare both the pullout face (X) and handle (Y) by rounding over the edges. Then attach the pullout face to the table with glue and screws through the face into the end caps. Secure the handle with 2" screws in counterbored holes to the pullout face.

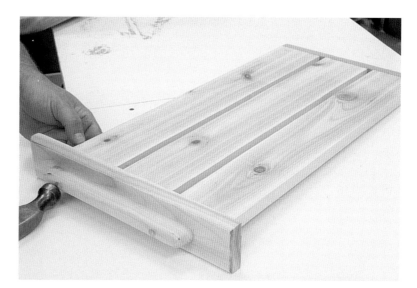

CONSTRUCTION NOTES

- Since this is a heavy piece of furniture, it will probably remain outdoors all summer. That's a good reason to use the best exterior-rated adhesives, hardware and finishes.

- The only other option that might be of value is a set of wheels. You can cut wooden wheels with a jigsaw, sand them smooth, and attach them to the front legs with carriage bolts as the axles. But if you don't plan to move your chaise a great deal, the wheels might not be necessary.

- You may also want a thin mattress for your chaise. If you're not skilled at sewing, you can enlist the help of a friend. However, don't leave the mattress on the chaise, as moisture will build up on the underside and eventually ruin the mattress and slats.

- This chaise is long and should accommodate even the tallest of people. But it can easily be altered to suit anyone's needs. Simply lengthen or shorten the main rails and adjust for the number of slats required.

- One of my friends saw the lounge and wanted one of her own. It illustrates how popular this project will be with friends and family. You may be building a few, so keep that leg pattern handy.

17 Install a stop cleat (Z) to limit the travel of the pullout. Secure it to the underside of the pullout with screws about 14" back from the front. Finally, complete the final sanding and apply a good exterior paint or stain. I used Sikkens Cetol 1 #078 Natural to complete my chaise lounge.

hammock stand

It seems the hammock was invented around 450 B.C. and encountered by Christopher Columbus when he landed in the West Indies in the late 15th century. And while most of us would like to have a hammock in our backyard, very few of us have two strong trees in the right location. Well, here's the solution!

This project is made from construction-grade cedar. Although it does use a lot of wood, it's very cost-effective when compared to commercial stands. I've also designed it to come apart for storage. Those of you who live in warmer climates can assemble the stand with glue and hardware; but if you live in a changing climate, you'll be concerned about storage. The beam is the most awkward piece, even when dismantled, but you should be able to tuck it away in the rafters of your garage.

The stand is very sturdy. I've had about 300 pounds in the hammock, which deflected the beam, but it held perfectly. I don't suggest you put that much weight on the hammock all the time, but it has that capacity.

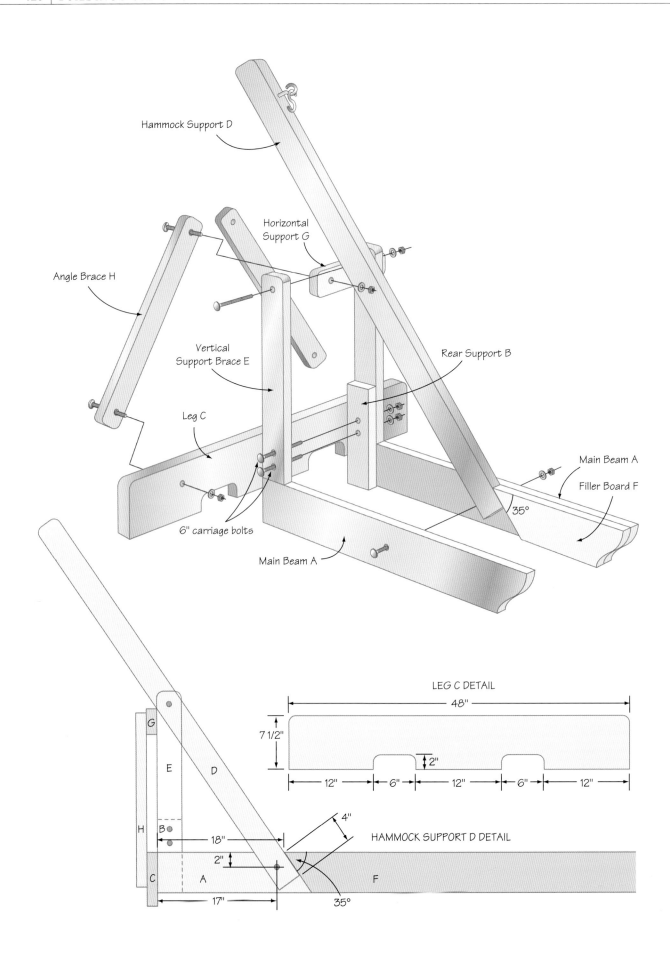

Hammock Support D

Horizontal Support G

Angle Brace H

Vertical Support Brace E

Rear Support B

Leg C

Main Beam A

Filler Board F

6" carriage bolts

Main Beam A

35°

LEG C DETAIL

48"

7 1/2"

2"

12"   6"   12"   6"   12"

4"

HAMMOCK SUPPORT D DETAIL

G

E   D

H   B

18"

2"

C   A   F

17"

35°

CUTTING LIST • **hammock stand**

REF.	QTY.	PART	MATERIAL	THICK	WIDTH	LENGTH	COMMENTS
A	2	Main beams	Cedar	$1\frac{1}{2}$	$5\frac{1}{2}$	168	
B	2	Rear supports	Cedar	$1\frac{1}{2}$	$3\frac{1}{2}$	10	
C	2	Legs	Cedar	$1\frac{1}{2}$	$7\frac{1}{2}$	48	
D	2	Hammock supports	Cedar	$1\frac{1}{2}$	$3\frac{1}{2}$	60	
E	4	Vertical support braces	Cedar	$1\frac{1}{2}$	$3\frac{1}{2}$	22	
F	1	Filler board	Cedar	$1\frac{1}{2}$	$5\frac{1}{2}$	$131\frac{1}{2}$	
G	2	Horizontal supports	Cedar	$1\frac{1}{2}$	$3\frac{1}{2}$	10	
H	4	Angle braces	Cedar	$1\frac{1}{2}$	$3\frac{1}{2}$	28	

Hardware and Supplies

$2\frac{1}{2}$" Exterior-rated screws

$\frac{3}{8}$"-dia. x 6" galvanized carriage bolts and nuts

$\frac{3}{8}$"-dia. x 5" galvanized carriage bolts and nuts

$\frac{3}{8}$"-dia. x 3" galvanized carriage bolts

Polyurethane glue

Sikkens Cetol I #996 Natural Light finish

REQUIRED **tools**

Table Saw or Circular Saw

Drill

Miter Box

Combination Square

Hammer

Screw Gun or Drivers

Jigsaw

Socket Wrenches

Sander or Sandpaper and Block

Router and Bits

Tip

When I was researching this project I dropped by the Hatteras Hammocks Web site (see "Sources"). They've got a great deal of information about hammocks and some interesting trivia.

1 Prepare the two main beams (A) by rounding over one face on each with a ½" roundover bit in a router. This rounded face will be the outside surface when constructing the stand's main beam. Cut the two rear supports (B). Miter the corners on one end of each board at 45°. The miter cuts are ½" in from the corner intersection. Use a belt sander to create a rounded top. Then, ease the edges of both faces with a ⅜" roundover bit. Then as shown here, install the supports in between and flush with both ends of the main beams. Use glue and four 2½" exterior-rated screws per side to secure the supports.

2 Cut notches in the two rear legs (C) as shown. Remove the sharp upper corners with a belt sander to prevent injuries. Finally, use a ⅜" roundover bit to soften both faces of the legs.

3 Attach the legs to the main beam with two ⅜"-diameter by 6"-long galvanized carriage bolts at each joint. Center the legs on the beam and flush with the top edge of the legs. Drill two ⅜" holes through the center of the legs and rear supports. If you don't want to make your hammock stand a knockdown model, you can use two lag bolts and adhesive at this joint. The same procedure will apply to all the other joints where I've used carriage bolts and nuts.

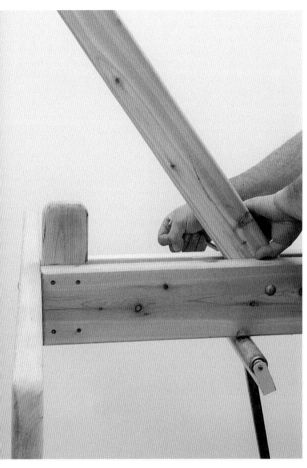

4 Cut the two hammock supports (D) to size and round over one end following the same procedure as completed on the rear supports. Round over both faces with a ⅜" roundover bit in a router. Install the supports between the main beams with a 35° back slant. Use a 5"-long carriage bolt through the beam and support to secure the joint.

5 The vertical support braces (E) are prepared in the same manner as the other pieces. Round over one end with a belt sander and ease both faces with a ⅜" roundover router bit. Use two ⅜" diameter by 5"-long carriage bolts through the rear support and one through the hammock support. The support braces are aligned vertically, flush with the rear support edges

6 Cut and install a filler board (F) between the two main beams. It's angle-cut at 35° on both ends to fit against the hammock supports. My filler measured 131½" to the longest points of the angles on both ends. However, check the exact measurement on your stand before cutting this board. Place it between and flush with the two main beams. Secure it with glue and 2½" screws every 12".

7 The two horizontal supports (G) require both ends rounded over on each board. As well, round over both faces on each with a ⅜" roundover bit. Use glue and four 2½" screws to secure these supports to the vertical supports. Position these horizontal supports tightly against the hammock supports.

8 Cut and round over the four angle braces (H). They are attached to the horizontal supports and legs with 3"-long galvanized carriage bolts. You will be required to counterbore a hole for the washers and nuts. Align the top corners of the angle braces with the outside top corners of the horizontal supports. The bottoms are attached to the legs with their outside corners 4¾" in from the leg ends.

9 My hammock hardware requirements needed an eyebolt and S-hook at the top of the hammock supports. However, the hammock you plan to use may be different, so check the requirements before completing this step. If you've built the knockdown version of this stand, it's worth dismantling before applying a finish. I finished my stand with Sikkens Cetol 1 #996 Natural Light.

CONSTRUCTION NOTES

- This hammock stand project seems fairly simple, but a great deal of design work was involved. I wanted a lighter-looking main beam, so I cut notches similar to those in the legs. That weakened the beam, and the deflection with a load in the hammock was so great that the ends of the stand lifted off the ground. The middle of the beam bent to the ground and pivoted the stand.

- I attempted to use a lighter beam of 2x4s but the deflection was too great. I also designed and built a stand with 5½"-wide legs that meant the main beam touched the ground. That also caused deflection and raised both ends.

- The stand detailed here is the final result of all the designing and prototypes. The stand needs 7½"-wide lumber for the legs and a multiple 2x6 beam system, raised off the ground, to perform properly. What first appeared to be a simple design process turned out to be very complicated. However, this final model is perfect.

- One final issue to consider might be the choice of wood. A hardwood deflects less than cedar or any other softwood, so that might be an option if the budget will allow the extra expense. But the softwoods do work fine with this design.

- Use glue and screws to join the two main beams, as well as the filler. They will form a massive beam that will be strong and resist deflection. You will still see main beam deflection with a heavy person in the hammock, but it won't be enough to cause any problems.

sources

Many suppliers contributed products, material and technical support during the project building phase. I appreciate how helpful they've been and recommend these companies without hesitation.

Adams & Kennedy
Manotick, Ontario
(613) 822-6800
www.adams-kennedy.com
Wood supply

Delta International
www.deltawoodworking.com

Hatteras Hammocks
Greenville, North Carolina
(800) 643-3522
www.hatham.com
Hammocks

House of Tools
Edmonton, Alberta
(800) 661-3987
www.houseoftools.com
Woodworking tools and hardware

JessEm Tool Company
Penetanguishene, Ontario
(800) 436-6799
www.jessem.com
Rout-R-Slide and Rout-R-Lift

Para Paints
Brampton, Ontario
(800) 461-7272
Sikkens Wood Finishes

Porter-Cable
Jackson, Tennessee
(800) 487-8665
www.porter-cable.com
Woodworking tools

Richelieu Hardware
Ville St-Laurent, Quebec
(800) 361-6000
www.richelieu.com
Hardware supplies to the professional trade

Rockler Woodworking and Hardware
Medina, Minnesota
(800) 279-4441
www.rockler.com
Woodworking tools and hardware

Sikkens Decorative Wood Finishes
Troy, Michigan
(800) 833-7288
www.sikkens.com
Wood finishes

Tenryu America
Melbourne, Florida
(800) 951-7297
www.tenryu.com
Saw blades

Tool Trend
Concord, Ontario
(800) 387-7005
www.tooltrend.com
Woodworking tools and hardware

Uncommon Goods
Guelph, Ontario
(519) 824-9612
Hammocks

Wolfcraft Inc.
Itasca, Illinois
(630) 773-4777
www.wolfcraft.com
Woodworking hardware

Woodcraft Supply Corp.
Parkersburg, West Virginia
(800) 225-1153
www.woodcraft.com
Woodworking hardware

Woodworker's Hardware
Sauk Rapids, Minnesota
(800) 383-0130
www.wwhardware.com
Woodworking hardware

index

A
Aliphatic resin glue, 13

B
Benches
    classic garden bench, 40-47
    curved planter bench, 48-55
    planter bench, 28-33
    tête-à-tête bench, 76-83
Biscuit joints, 15
Board foot, 10

C
Cedar, 10
Chaise lounge, 108-117
Classic garden bench, 40-47
Classic picnic table, 92-97
Construction adhesives, 14
Corner privacy screen, 34-39
Curved planter bench, 48-55

D
Dado joints, 15
Dining set, outdoor, 84-91
Dry wood, 10

E
Elegant planter, 22-27
Epoxy resin glue, 13-14

F
Finishing
    don'ts, 14-15
    do's, 14-15
    tips, 14
Folding side table, 56-61
Formal side table, 68-75

G
Glues
    aliphatic resin glue, 13
    choices, 14
    construction adhesives, 14
    epoxy resin glue, 13-14
    plastic resin marine glue, 13
    polyurethane glue, 13
Grading, wood, 10
Green wood, 10

H
Hammock stand, 118-125
Hardware

hot-dipped galvanized, 12
    outdoor screws, 12
    stainless steel, 12
Horizontal panel planter, 16-21
Hot-dipped galvanized hardware, 12

J
Joinery
    biscuit joints, 15
    dado joints, 15
    mortise-and-tenon joints, 15

L
Lumber. *see* Wood, generally

M
Mahogany, 10-11
Mortise-and-tenon joints, 15

O
Oak, white, 11
Octagonal table, 98-107
Outdoor coffee table, 62-67
Outdoor dining set, 84-91

P
Picnic table, classic, 92-97
Pine, 12
Planters
    bench, curved planter, 48-55
    bench, planter, 28-33
    curved planter bench, 48-55
    elegant planter, 22-27
    horizontal panel planter, 16-21
Plastic resin marine glue, 13
Plastic wood, 11-12
Polyurethane glue, 13
Pressure-treated wood, 11
Privacy screen, corner, 34-39
Projects
    chaise lounge, 108-117
    classic garden bench, 40-47
    classic picnic table, 92-97
    corner privacy screen, 34-39
    curved planter bench, 48-55
    elegant planter, 22-27
    folding side table, 56-61
    formal side table, 68-75
    hammock stand, 118-125
    horizontal panel planter, 16-21
    octagonal table, 98-107
    outdoor coffee table, 62-67

outdoor dining set, 84-91
    planter bench, 28-33
    tête-à-tête bench, 76-83
Properties of wood, 10

R
Redwood, 10

S
Safety issues, wood, 10
Sanding tips, 14
Screen, corner privacy, 34-39
Screws, outdoor, 12
Species of wood, 10-12
Stainless steel hardware, 12

T
Tables
    classic picnic table, 92-97
    folding side table, 56-61
    formal side table, 68-75
    octagonal table, 98-107
    outdoor coffee table, 62-67
Teak, 11
Tête-à-tête bench, 76-83

W
White oak, 11
Wood
    board foot, 10
    cedar, 10
    dry wood, 10
    grading, 10
    green wood, 10
    mahogany, 10-11
    oak, white, 11
    pine, 12
    plastic wood, 11-12
    pressure-treated wood, 11
    properties, 10
    redwood, 10
    safety issues, 10
    species, 10-12
    teak, 11
    white oak, 11

The Best Woodworking Projects From Popular Woodworking Books

Classic Country Furniture
Packed with 20 attractive and functional projects, this guide provides you with the perfect mix of techniques, woods and designs for building country furniture. Fully illustrated steps and instructions accompany each piece, so you can complete projects without any guesswork.
#70475/$19.99/128 pages/250 color images/paperback

Authentic Arts & Crafts Furniture Projects
Whatever your skill level, you'll find something special in this beautifully crafted book. Each classic furniture project is taken from the files of *Popular Woodworking*, the skill-building project magazine for practical woodworkers.
#70499/$24.99/128 pages/200 color images/paperback

How to Build Classic Garden Furniture
This easy, step-by-step guide will have you anxious to begin crafting this elegant outdoor furniture. The 20 projects are designed to withstand years of outdoor exposure with minimal care, and are versatile enough to complement any home's style. Each beautiful piece is made easy to accomplish with full-color illustrations, numbered steps, close-up photos and alternatives for design, wood selection and finishing.
#70395/$24.99/128 pages/275 color, 69 b&w illus./paperback

Make Your Own Jigs & Woodshop Furniture
Innovative jigs and fixtures will help you specialize your ordinary power tools without spending big money. You'll get plans for over 40 jigs and fixtures, 23 projects for a well-outfitted workshop and more!
#70249/$24.99/144 pages/100 b&w, 100 color illus.

Quick & Easy Furniture You Can Build with Dimensional Lumber
This book ensures that you get the most for your money when it comes to purchasing and building with framing lumber. It covers every aspect of the furniture-making process with step-by-step instructions, precise measurements, full-color photos, tips and sidebars.
#70459/$22.99/128 pages/250 color images/paperback

Classic Arts & Crafts Furniture You Can Build
In this guide, you'll find 20 step-by-step projects for every room in your home. Suitable for all woodworkers—even beginners—each of these projects is a gorgeous representation of the Arts & Crafts style.
#70422/$24.99/128 pages/69 color, 30 b&w illus./paperback

Smart Shelving & Storage Solutions
These innovative and inexpensive storage solutions are perfect for do-it-yourselfers. From book shelves, chests and cabinets to armoires, closet systems and benches, you'll find more than 27 woodworking projects to help you make the most of your space—whether it's under the bed, over the sink or in the garage.
#70445/$24.99/144 pages/360 color, 40 b&w illus./paperback

The Weekend Woodworker
A fantastic resource for the straightforward, step-by-step projects you like! This book offers you a range of attractive challenges, from smaller items—such as a stylish CD rack, mailbox or birdhouse—to larger, easy-to-assemble projects including a wall cupboard, child's bed, computer workstation or coffee table. Each project provides clear and easy step-by-step instructions, photographs and diagrams, ideal for both the beginner and expert.
#70456/$22.99/144 pages/200 color photos/paperback

Display Cabinets You Can Customize
Go beyond building to designing furniture. You'll receive step-by-step instructions to the base projects—the starting points for a wide variety of pieces, such as display cabinets, tables and cases. Then you'll learn about customizing techniques. You'll see how to adapt a glass-front cabinet; put a profile on a cabinet by using moulding; get a different look by using stained glass or changing the legs and much more!
#70282/$18.99/128 pages/150 b&w illus./paperback

25 Essential Projects for Your Workshop
This collection contains some of the most popular projects from *Popular Woodworking* magazine! Each one has been designed for practical use in the wood shop—clever stands, cabinets, storage devices and more. In addition, helpful "shop tips" are sprinkled throughout each chapter, providing invaluable insight and advice.
#70472/$22.99/128 pages/275 color images/paperback

How to Design and Build Your Ideal Woodshop
Designed especially for the home-shop woodworker, this guide features dozens of practical alternatives, tips and solutions for transforming attics, garages, basements or out-buildings into efficient and safe woodshops. Clear instructions also include photos, drawings and considerations for electricity, lighting, ventilation, plumbing, accessibility, insulation, flooring and more.
#70397/$24.99/160 pages/paperback

Good Wood Handbook, Second Edition
Now in paperback! This handy reference gives you all the information you need to select and use the right wood for the job—before you buy. You'll discover valuable information on a wide selection of commercial softwoods and hardwoods—from common uses, color and grain to how the wood glues and takes finish.
#70451/$14.99/128 pages/250 color illus./paperback

Woodworker's Guide to Selecting and Milling Wood
Save money on lumber as you preserve the great tradition of felling, milling and drying your own wood. Loads of full-color illustrations will help you identify the right wood for every job.
#70248/$22.99/144 pages/128 b&w illus., 32 color photos

Other fine Popular Woodworking Books are available from your local bookstore or direct from the publisher. Write to the address below for a FREE catalog of all Popular Woodworking Books. To order books directly from the publisher, include $3.95 postage and handling for one book, $1.95 for each additional book. Ohio residents add 6% sales tax. Allow 30 days for delivery.

Popular Woodworking Books
4700 East Galbraith Road
Cincinnati, Ohio 45236
VISA/MasterCard orders call TOLL-FREE
1-800-289-0963

Prices subject to change without notice. Stock may be limited on some books.